Additional Praise for

The
Madwoman
in the
Volvo

"Reads like a weekend away with the best friend you ever had—blazingly vulnerable, scorchingly smart, and funny as hell. It's both an intimate portrait of one woman as she approaches menopause and a full-throated cultural howl about what it means to be female and forty or fifty or sixty-something in America today. I was filled with recognition as I read the book's first pages and flooded with gratitude by the end. . . . A beautiful book you're going to miss after you've read the last page."

—Cheryl Strayed, author of *Wild*

"[Reading this book] I laughed maniacally, nodded in empathy, hooted, teared up, and laughed some more. And while you could make the case that with a menopausal woman, that could have happened even had I spent the time gardening, in this case I am pretty certain it was the author's doing."

—Mary Roach, author of *Gulp*

"Performer-humorist Loh isn't going crazy. She is heading straight into menopause, and her experiences and thoughts on the topic are hilarious, comforting, and enlightening. . . . Loh has cleared this treacherous, necessary path with her own wildly humorous story, a few facts here and there, and her funny and eye-opening summations of advice from the many change-of-life books she has plowed through. . . . Misery may never prove better company." —*Booklist*

"Loh is that rare writer who is howlingly funny on the surface and subtly brilliant just beneath. Here, she turns her eagle eye to her own midlife 'crises': motherhood, marriage, men (old and young), and madness of all kinds—not least her own. Goes down like cheap wine—fast and furiously—yet at the end, instead of a hangover, you have a bold and beautiful new view of life."

—Cathi Hanauer, author of
Gone and editor of *The Bitch in the House*

"Chock-a-block full of great advice, Loh's talent for storytelling makes this laugh-out-loud memoir extremely memorable. She not only cuts to the chase but she chases away any notions you might have had about menopause while making you feel like you might just live through the craziness that hormonal hell can bestow upon a woman. Unputdownable and unparalleled in wit and wisdom; this one's a must read." —*Dish Mag*

"If I had to experience the calamity that is perimenopause without Sandra Tsing Loh's wise and witty model, I'm not sure I would make it through in one piece. (My family certainly wouldn't.) Ms. Loh possesses an eviscerating insight into the perils of this often tumultuous stage of life, but more importantly, she's hilariously funny. *Madwoman in the Volvo* left me giggling on the couch, thrilled to be ignoring my children for the good reason of being immersed in a delicious and marvelous book."   —Ayelet Waldman, author of *Bad Mother*

The
Madwoman
in the
Volvo

The
Madwoman
in the
Volvo

MY YEAR OF RAGING HORMONES

Sandra Tsing Loh

W. W. NORTON & COMPANY

New York • London

For information about permission to reproduce selections from this book,
write to Permissions, W. W. Norton & Company, Inc., 500 Fifth Avenue,
New York, NY 10110

For information about special discounts for bulk purchases, please
contact W. W. Norton Special Sales at specialsales@wwnorton.com or
800-233-4830

Manufacturing by Courier Westford
Book design by Ellen Cipriano
Production manager: Anna Oler

ISBN: 978-0-393-08868-7

W. W. Norton & Company, Inc.
500 Fifth Avenue, New York, N.Y. 10110
www.wwnorton.com
W. W. Norton & Company Ltd.
Castle House, 75/76 Wells Street, London W1T 3QT

ISBN 978-0-393-35109-5 pbk.

1 2 3 4 5 6 7 8 9 0

For my mother,
Gisela, and all the world's other
fabulous Madwomen

Contents

The
Madwoman
in the
Volvo

Prologue:
Gloomings

I'M HURTLING WEST ALONG the 101 Freeway to the Valley to pick my daughters up from school. I am forty-nine years old, and I have just gotten off the phone with my friend and magazine editor, Ben. We have been talking about refinancing: It's a wonderfully mundane topic of conversation—one of those truly harmless pleasures of midlife. It helps me to recall not all, but at least some, of the staid, rational person I was not too long ago: which is to say before I, a forty-something suburban mother, became involved in a wild and ill-considered extramarital affair.

"Listen," Ben says excitedly. "I know two years ago John Warick got you that thirty years fixed at 4.75 percent, which as we know is historically unheard of. But I'm telling you, this new guy who's doing my next refinance, at Wells Fargo? When I ran your numbers by him, he thought you could qualify for an even lower thirty years fixed like . . . 4.275." Ben is as much of a math nerd about this stuff as I am.

Indeed, under normal circumstances, I am the sort of

OCD person for whom the number 4.275 would create a spike of excitement. It's the same adrenaline rush I get when successfully completing a newspaper sudoku or crossword puzzle with a sharp number 2 pencil. Ben and I can get truly wound up around our small personal-finance triumphs most of the time. But today even this conversation hasn't supplied its usual lift. I find myself feeling surprisingly flat.

Until now, not being able to feel things has never been one of my copious personal flaws. I am, for better or for worse, a person obsessively driven by passions large and small. I find my mind drifting to dinner. I remember in that moment that I promised my girls that morning that tonight's dinner would be Make Your Own Pizza.

IN THEORY Make Your Own Pizza is one of the wonderfully creative new things my girls and I do. Now that my kids go back and forth between my ex-husband and me, I have periods of rest. As a consequence, I've been able to bring on an astonishing amount of high-quality parenting. Ironically, here is the artisanal attention and care I was never able to provide as a full-time mother. In our new life together in our big short-saled Victorian house, my girls and I make lemonade from scratch, bake pies, and paint Easter eggs. I've taught them to ride bikes, to crochet, and to paint on actual easels with watercolors. We even go bowling, and we have Make Your Own Pizza for dinner.

I find myself thinking ahead to the burned pizza stone

languishing crusty and unwashed in the oven. I think of how sticky the Trader Joe's dough is, of how I will probably need to get two kinds, the garlic-herb and the whole wheat. I think of how needlessly jam-packed the parking lot at Trader Joe's is in midafternoon, how surprisingly uninspired their samples— lukewarm cups of bland organic rotelli, cloudy vials of unfiltered apple juice. My feeling of flatness gives way decidedly, at the thought of Make Your Own Pizza, to sudden and dramatic gloom.

I hang up on Ben, pull off the freeway, and park under a tree in front of a dirty-yellow ranch-style house to collect myself and instead instantly begin sobbing, producing heaves of seawater like Jonah's whale. It's not just the pizza. Suddenly an image comes to me, seemingly at random, of my daughters' hamster. Because they are always begging for more pets, their dad had given them a toffee-blond hamster named Hammy, who stayed with me one weekend when they all went out of town. He spent the day as my little companion, happily rolling around in his blue plastic ball while I wrote at the computer. After Hammy went home I heard from the girls that he had gotten sick—"Probably from eating his own wood chips," Sally reported—and subsequently died.

Hunched over the steering wheel, I think—why now?— of that little face, those little paws, that jingling blue ball. I think of Hammy's sunny disposition and friendly, inquisitive nose, and his essential innocence and trueness and goodness. I am a forty-nine-year-old woman sitting in her filthy Volvo parked under a tree on a Tuesday afternoon wailing about a hamster. Just how low are we setting the bar here? (And yet, why of all things did God have to take this hamster? What was the harm?)

I want to call my older sister, Kaitlin, but I shouldn't. My sister and I are so close it's as if we share a limb. When Kaitlin and I are getting along, we talk all the time, and she gives the greatest, most amazing sister advice (call that Pema Chödrön, after the crop-haired Tibetan-Buddhist nun whose inspirational writings we both adore). When we are fighting I can almost physically feel the phone not ring, and it feels intentionally strategic (call that . . . Margaret Thatcher). But I've put Kaitlin through a hell of a lot. My affair almost killed her. After all, I'm not just her middle-aged kid sister but the mother of her two favorite nieces. No, I can't call her, because if she sensed I was going off the deep end again, Kaitlin would have to stage an intervention to treat the entire family.

Instead I find myself dialing Ann. Ann is not necessarily my closest girlfriend, but she is the most sensible and the longest happily married. (I've had my share of crazy girlfriends, and since my divorce it seems like everyone else's twenty-year-long marriages are now suddenly toppling over like dominoes. All these wild-eyed women want to meet for coffee, as though I'm a sort of underground-divorce-railroad Harriet Tubman, and the vibe is unsettling.) Ann is together. Ann always has a good plumber, contractor, or electrician. Ann knows which Beverly Hills specialist to call if you have a mysterious spot or rash. Ann has a beautifully organized shoe closet.

"Hello?" Ann says after two and a half rings. Barely able

to choke the words out, I tell her about my sorrow over the hamster, and about this sudden, violent stab of midafternoon midlife malaise.

She says: "Oh sweetie. I'm so sorry to hear that. Can I ask—when did you last have your period?"

"I have no idea. I can barely keep food in the fridge and my daughters in underwear."

"But might you have missed any?"

"Oh sure." I frown. Good God—who keeps track of periods anymore?

"I think . . . ? Maybe . . . ? Because it sounds so familiar . . . ? You may not want to hear this, but you could be entering menopause."

"Menopause?!" I cry out in relief. "Just menopause? That would be awesome! I thought I was going mad or something!"

But now Ann goes on to describe a personal daily routine that is about the most complicated one I have ever heard of. It is a rigorously titrated cocktail of antidepressants, bioidenticals, walks, facials, massages, dark chocolate, and practically throwing salt over the left shoulder.

"And it's most intense at that certain time of the month. That's when I have these bouts of progesterone depression balanced with rage—tons and tons of rage. I'm shouting on the streets, in traffic, at my husband. I almost killed someone in the parking lot at B of A. I can feel like I'm really going crazy. I throw things. For no reason. Weird things set me off. So just for those days—it's four to five days—I have to up my Estrovel. If I remember. The hardest thing is just to remember." She recommends her dream gynecologist, Dr. Valerie. I take the number without admitting that I'm not sure I'm ready to see a doctor, because quite frankly I can't face being weighed.

Later I'll go home to my laptop for a crash course in the history of the change. Wow—there's so much I didn't know. Menopause was first mentioned in ancient Greece by writers like Aristotle, who pegged both menstrual periods and fertility as ending at the same time for women, then around age forty. Cited in European scholarly texts in the Middle Ages, menopause took an unattractive turn in 1816 when the French physician Charles de Gardanne termed "ménopause" a nervous disorder. This no doubt contributed to medical thinking in the later 1800s that menopause was a time when a woman "ceased to exist for the species" and "resembled a dethroned queen" (these from a description of female diseases). The first complete book on menopause, with the warm and fuzzy title of *The Change of Life in Health and Disease* (1857), by John Edward Tilt, apparently cites 135 different menopause symptoms, including curious manifestations like pseudonarcotism, temporary deafness, uncontrollable peevishness, and "hysterical flatulence." Yikes!

By contrast, it appears that non-European cultures have more organic, female-friendly approaches to menopause. Mayan women famously report not having any negative menopausal symptoms at all. American Indian women and their faraway Chinese sisters have long treated menopausal symptoms with such healing natural remedies as angelica (dong quai). In India a woman's ascent into this next, nonmothering phase of life is seen as a sacred time of greater spiritual depth and exploration.

Instead of "ceasing to exist for the species," for Hindu women menopause opens the door to enlightenment, growth, and wisdom. As I'll learn in the chapters to come, enlightenment, growth, and wisdom are only part of the package.

AS ANN and I hang up, mostly I'm relieved at her diagnosis. As though a temporary fog has been blasted away with lemon-scented Febreze, I turn the key in the ignition, pick up my girls, go to Target, and follow that with Trader Joe's. Invigorated by this new information, I'm again rocking my chores. In the checkout line I fumble with keys, sunglasses, debit card, and change, as is increasingly common for me these days. I have this thing where if I forget my canvas bags, I feel so guilty about the harm that plastic wreaks on the planet that I stack all my groceries into my arms. Doubled over, I shuffle out to the car, leaving a trail of broken eggs, milk, cantaloupe.

"You need a hand, hon?" the female checker asks. "Oh no," I say. With a big smile I turn to the entire line behind me and grandly announce: "Don't mind me—I'm just forty-nine and entering *menopause*!"

Burning Woman

BUT THAT'S NOT WHERE the story of my midlife crisis begins.

Flashback to two years before. It's 9:00 A.M. on a blindingly bright Monday morning. I am forty-seven years old, in T-shirt and overalls. I am weeping as I hurl paperback after paperback into a clanging metal Dumpster in front of a U-Haul storage facility in Pasadena. This is my personal library, those familiar literary classics lovingly assembled in my salad days (college, grad school, etc.). It feels like sacrilege to toss them. It's a betrayal of the concrete blocks, then red milk crates, then black IKEA Billy bookshelves they once stood on. I am jettisoning into the trash all of art, and history, and goodness, and knowledge.

On the other hand, I appear to have no fewer than three separate copies of Gabriel García Márquez's *One Hundred Years of Solitude*. This is a book that, to be honest, I have never read and that, I now realize, I never plan to. I cannot even remember pretending to read it, though I must have been assigned it in a course (perhaps three times?). That's the case, too, with my moldering pile of Henry James, which I am also jettisoning.

I'm here at U-Haul on a blistering Monday morning because I've just been kicked out of my home of twenty years. My home, I see in retrospect, was a kind of Eden, a funky hippie enclave in a bucolic part of town, with two pools, a recording studio, and even a charmingly jerry-rigged home office overlooking a hot tub. That's where my library of unread books had room to loll sunnily, next to unused exercise equipment and unopened boxes of life-improving (one day!) things like TurboTax.

But all this has been packed up and labeled for me in cardboard boxes—forty-three of them—by my former husband, henceforward to be referred to as Mr. X. I drove the giant shuddering U-Haul truck back home one last time to retrieve the boxes, stacked six feet high, under a blue rain tarp on the driveway. There was so much stuff it didn't all fit into the truck: I left lamps, CDs, and wedding platters scattered along the sidewalk.

It wasn't supposed to end this way. For such a long time our union was happy and solid. Mr. X and I met two decades ago, in Los Angeles. I was twenty-six and at a crossroads. Raised by a Chinese engineer father and a German mother in 1970s suburban Southern California, I had been shuttled to constant piano and ballet lessons with the middle-class idea that these would be nice hobbies to complement a sensible future job in aerospace engineering. But after struggling to earn a degree in physics and then moonlighting for six years in English graduate school (to my father's horror), I had veered offtrack: I wanted to be an artist. What sort of artist I had no clue—I played the

piano and composed and wrote and danced and painted and
did performance art. I was miserable at all of that, and miserable at being single. I had this dinosaur DNA code that if I
had any intimate relations with a man, I would be on his front
porch the next morning with packed suitcases, a coffeemaker,
and big puppy eyes.

I was lucky then to meet Mr. X, a friend of a friend. Somewhat but not crushingly older than I (eight years), Mr. X was a
well-regarded and fully employed studio musician. From a
musical family, he had played scales for hours a day from the
time he was a boy in Minnesota, and to him making music was
as natural as breathing. Mr. X was disciplined about his craft,
and as we started to date and he learned of my creative aspira-
tions, he insisted I also be. Crying was not allowed, even if I
had a short story rejected sixty times. ("Do you know how
many auditions I didn't get?" he would exclaim. "Get up on your
feet, girl!") He pushed me to leave my freshman-teaching-and-
dodging-my-thesis-adviser grad-school safety zone and approach
art like a job. Mr. X was a good person, a grown-up, and a
romantic. In summer backyards we drank wine and ate barbecue, listened to Miles Davis, smoked pot, and played Scrabble.
He praised me for being—as opposed to his ex—"un-neurotic,"
a trait I tried to work hard to maintain.

We soon bought a home together, thanks to his income
and a loan from my family. Now on our own patch of earth,
our roots grew down. On his own land Mr. X turned out to
be very much a homebody—if not actually a farmer, as I used
to joke. When not on the road, he roasted chickens, baked

bread, and grew tomatoes. He hung laundry, hired painters, and installed showerheads. He mended fences, serviced cars, bought insurance. I dug into my writing and began publishing essays, short stories, and even books about what I called the foibles of my generation, and I started to tell coherent stories onstage instead of doing unintelligible performance-art pieces. I soon had so much to do that when Mr. X went on tour, as he often did, I missed him less and less. We both felt this was a good development, as in the early days my overattachment was unmanageable—I used to wail in alarmed grief whenever he went away.

Eventually there comes the day, a decade in, when, returning from a several-month tour, he puts his bags down on the front porch, looks up, and the first words out of his mouth are not "How are you?" but "The roof needs retiling." When I see him in another room folding laundry and laughing till tears come at *The Daily Show*, I realize I haven't seen him laugh like that at anything I've said in years. When we go to dinner for "date night" and can't fill more than forty-five minutes of conversation, I know it's because we have become so unfamiliar with each other's worlds.

But the loss of Mr. X is not why I am weeping at this moment, as I continue to toss out classic after classic this morning in rhythmic arcs of grief (Hemingway, Melville, Trollope— *thunk, thunk, thunk*). I'm weeping because we were supposed to be . . . doing this . . . together.

But by "we" I mean myself and Mr. Y. And there you go. Life's next wrinkle.

. . .

I'D MET Mr. Y a decade before. I was in need of a manager
for my theater work, and that's when my director introduced
us. Mr. Y was a funny, smart, theater gypsy like the rest of us,
but he was a businessperson who calmly took care of the vexing
stuff like contracts, and budgets, and 1099s. Mr. Y was fun
to have around, either in the theater or on the road. An old-
fashioned flaneur with a different tie, hat, or polished boot for
every occasion, he had endless patience for shopping, browsing,
café sitting. Of Scotch-Irish blood and WASP training, Mr. Y
was a fellow always happy to duck into a pub for a nightcap,
and he was also a gentleman glad to chivalrously hold open the
door. At opening-night parties, when I was marooned, excitedly but rather anxiously holding court before a group of the-
atergoers, he'd arrive magically by my side with not one but
two calming cocktails ("Irish handcuffs"). "Life in wartime!"
he'd say.

THE FACT that Mr. Y and I were both in stable long-term
marriages with children—he had a twenty-one-year-old son,
and I had two young daughters—put us at ease together. We
soon developed a platonic friendship that was as comfortable
as an old shoe. As his French architect wife seemed to travel
as much as Mr. X did, we increasingly kept each other company in that affable midlife beer garden of our forties. Sharing

a business checking account, we were buddies in work and in life. He was the Ethel to my Lucy.

MY PROFESSIONAL focus was shifting, too. One day when I was forty-two, Mr. X and I attended a crowded open house for a fancy potential private kindergarten for our older daughter. We couldn't afford the $20K-plus tuition, but neither could we choose public school, as our local public schools were terrible, or so we had been told. But this ambivalence quickly resolved itself. The smug director of admissions answered a parent's question with: "But *no* one goes to public school in Los Angeles!" When I realized that by "no one" this man was referring to approximately 750,000 children, I knew that I had found my passion and my cause.

All my life I had worked for myself, alone, on narrow intellectual projects, in what I now understood to be a shallow, self-centered void. But now, on behalf of 750,000 children, I could cut the rope to my past and dedicate myself to something *huge*!!! I could join the *world*!!! It turned out that I was but one of many educated, middle-class Los Angeles moms who felt this way. (There had been kind of a baby boom triggered around 9/11, so there were many of us who had toddlers at the same time.) We had all been sleepwalking through our thirties, pursuing less-than-meaningful careers, writing condo association newsletters, and accumulating many sets of wicker furniture, which we had then dutifully painted with sealant. But around forty, awakening to the needs of our and the world's children, our hormones were sailing as high as in our teens. We, the

Burning Moms, were going to save the world by fomenting a public-education revolution.

At the apex of my mania I decided to throw a massive public-school rally in Sacramento. At this point Mr. X was starting to look askance at all of his wife's frenetic activity as one would look askance at Don Quixote tilting at windmills. A former performance artist himself, however, Mr. Y, unlike Mr. X, found my activities perfectly reasonable. He even agreed to drive a twenty-seven-foot U-Haul housing a gigantic papier-mâché elephant up to Sacramento. It is a measure of how much I took him for granted that I never doubted Mr. Y would do such a thing, if asked.

This political rally was, unfortunately, more a ragtag multifamily outing than a politically effective transformative event. As I've learned since, real change involves more than stenciling banners rhapsodically in the sun with one's children. But still I felt I'd been a part of something magical. The night before the rally, one hundred women and children had camped together in firelight, and I poked my head into row after row of gaily flapping tents to give my soldiers cheery huzzahs. Less Joan of Arc, I was a mother on fire.

OUR NEXT adventure was more in the spirit of fun, not protest. The simple act of RV camping proved so liberating for several Burning Moms, who were starting to sport aviator sunglasses and bandannas, that we decided we were now badass enough to hazard a trip to Burning Man. Which is where the magic flipped upside down.

Burning Man is an annual pagan, clothing-optional, drug-friendly weeklong gathering of some fifty thousand people who build a temporary city in the scorching Nevada desert. It was an unlikely destination for a suburban middle-aged mother such as myself. But the year before, Mr. X, in his constant search for offbeat movies on Netflix, had found a documentary focusing less on the culture of Burning Man than on its spectacular art. Mr. X and I watched in genuine wonder. Wow! Here were giant metal dune buggies and alien-spaceship-inspired flame-throwers and even a fairy-tale-like wooden temple into which people threw whatever they wished to get rid of, from wedding dresses to letters from dead wastrel fathers, which was then burned to the ground. For a moment Mr. X and I had considered going, but given that he was a fifty-something-year-old dad who had long given up all of his youthful bad habits (including not just pot but alcohol)—whereas, of course, somewhat furtively, I myself had not—we mutually and sensibly let the idea fizzle.

However, now that I had formed this tribe of Burning Moms, we could go as a she-wolf pack and take pictures. And for protection we would take not just Clinique moisturizer but our mascot and driver, Mr. Y. Breathed Mr. X, "A male chaperone. Yes. Thank goodness."

Burning Man turned out to be a lot how you'd expect a desert "city" of half-nude stoners to be, particularly stoners who had built makeshift "camps" with names like Andy's Wonder Factory, Astral Headwash, Big Puffy Yellow Camp, Barbie Deathcamp and Wine Bistro, A Shack of Sit, and Zombie Unicorn. Ours was called Camp Baggage Check ("Check your emotional baggage at the door"), a relatively normal camp run by a software engineer from the Pacific Northwest. Reassured by such ordinary recreational totems as Doritos, beer, and dominoes, our group of six felt ourselves slow down and relax into the heat. We women gradually stripped down to our shorts and flip-flops and even bikini tops. There was no fear of appearing fat or of even being looked at twice at all by the sixty-something-year-old men rattling past naked on bicycles (ouch!). Feeling as though we were falling into a pleasant, heavy dream, my friend Lily and I set out for an exploratory stroll around the sandy metropolis' grand central circular boulevard.

As lulling as the drone of midafternoon bees, our conversation began with chitchat about our families. Lily was married to Brian, and they were the parents of Nick. Together they were the quintessential comfortable alterna-family—they barbecued, brewed their own beer, and hosted a funny Christmas-caroling party that always featured antlers on pets and kazoos. They had a bungalow in Silver Lake. Their son was in a wonderful new homegrown charter school, and they had a wonderful dog. Lily and I were making plans for our fall "Martinis and Magnets" (where we would ply anxious parents with martinis as we explained LA's frighteningly complex magnet-school system). It was in the middle of this conversation that Lily turned to me and asked: "You know what I'm going to get myself for my forty-fifth birthday?"

"What?" I said.

She leaned back, opened her chest to the heavens, and said: "An affair."

"What?"

It was like that moment in *Jaws* when Roy Scheider hears his first "shark" scream and the background wipes into ribbons. It was the moment you so wish you hadn't heard what you heard. You would give everything to throw that ugly horned toadfish back into the pond, never to be seen again.

Lily began to tell me about a traveling LAUSD (Los Angeles Unified School District) theater instructor at her kid's school—oh the cliché, and oh the irony, given that her husband was also a theater instructor. She was clearly merely bored with the good things she already had, and wanted to start over with something similar. "The thing is that Simon and I realize we both have this background in world theater," Lily was chattering on, "so we've started having coffee, to strategize how to bring the work of Augusto Boal to school. But then Simon sends me this e-mail with this Pablo Neruda poem! And I'm thinking, oh my God, he really likes me, and now we have this dinner date next week for Indian food. . . ."

No, no, no. I wanted Lily to be my funny sensible-mom girlfriend who enjoyed wine and gossip. I did not want her to reject her wonderful family life—and, by extension, mine—for a secretive sex life with a traveling LAUSD theater teacher.

Against my will Lily continued. "And I realized how you can know someone for years and then all of a sudden something causes you to see them in this totally different way. It hadn't occurred to me to have an affair—I'd just resigned myself to the fact that I'd never have sex again because Brian is now interested only in his online historical baseball league, you know—. And of course I've had this yeast infection. But now that we're here at Burning Man and people are so free, I just want to go back home and grab my life!" And with that she removed her top and tied it around her neck like a scarf! Oh Jesus! And in that vast hallucinogenic trailer park, even this awkward moment passed unnoticed.

And yet all at once I found myself thinking about Mr. Y. I'd always considered him conventionally attractive, surely, if I even thought about it, which I never did. He was my buddy—in truth, we were really more like girlfriends. But now I suddenly felt—and this is how addled your mind gets in the desert, which is why you really need to keep hydrating—that, given our ten-year-long platonic friendship, it might be nice to grab a quick camp snuggle with my good friend Mr. Y. It would be akin to affectionately rubbing the ears of a favorite golden retriever. With his irreverent Scotch-Irish sense of humor and WASP discretion, Mr. Y could be depended on to take a snuggle in the proper safe and convivial spirit. And we did in fact have a business relationship. Which surely boded well for this little idea of mine. Didn't it?

My fists flew to the sides of my face in hot confusion as Lily kept going on. No, no, no! What was I thinking? Both Mr. Y and I were happily married with children—so happily married that both of our extremely tolerant spouses had encouraged us to go to Burning Man and to have fun! And it wasn't as if I had to satisfy the ragings of my libido, which I hadn't noticed in years.

A couple of hours later I found myself nudging Mr. Y in the elbow in a collegial way and saying, "Can you believe it? Lily has gone mad in the desert heat. She's thinking of having an affair back in LA with her son's traveling LAUSD theater teacher." I decided that, to sublimate the confused state Lily's confession had left me in, I would not commit an actual adulterous deed but the next best thing: I would gossip about one. It would have a frisson of danger, but it would be entirely contextualized and safe.

"Oh God, that's never a good idea," he said, adjusting his improvised-for-the-desert sarong. "Why?"

"Well," I replied, "she says sometimes you can know someone for a long time and one day see him a totally different way." And then I heard myself saying something like: "And I now do similarly realize, Mr. Y, that I think you're hot, I guess I'm sort of madly in love with you, have been ever since I first laid eyes on you ten years ago, but you were so married and unavailable with your flat affect, and so was I, which is why we've been best friends for a decade and each other's constant companions, but as in a tragic Merchant-Ivory movie nothing will ever happen because we are married to others, and suddenly in midlife I see all I have lost and now excuse me while I go hurl my youth into the fire!"

Mr. Y and I had known each other so long I wasn't even particularly embarrassed to have said this. I had spontaneously blurted out this spate of truth, and there was nothing more to do but gaze at this thought balloon and watch it blow away into the cloudless desert sky. There it went, like a dandelion, disappearing over the low brown hills. So I loved him—how interesting that it had turned out that at forty-six I wasn't entirely done. There was one last man on earth I truly wanted to sleep with. In a moment, perhaps, this desire would be gone, forgotten, and on Sunday the temple, with its dead letters and wedding dresses, would be burned. Then Monday would be Monday. Tuesday would be Tuesday. Life would continue as usual because my youth was over. The cat would poop in her litter box, the cars would need servicing, there would be—always—something very good on HBO.

Oh my God, I thought. I finally understand that Prufrock poem: "I grow old . . . I grow old . . . / I shall wear the bottom of my trousers rolled."

But in the inky blackness just a few hours later, the towering Burning Man fell in flames to the desert floor. And now Mr. Y had had time to think it over. If I loved him, it turned out my feelings weren't entirely unrequited. If I wanted out of my marriage, so did he. It was part of a vague grand plan. "I always figured we'd end up together eventually, like in our sixties or seventies," Mr. Y said.

And so we made a prison break for it.

We dug ourselves out of our cells with spoons, and we ran for it.

Which is to say that Mr. Y and I exploded into a second adolescence. We were like pirates. We smoked, drank, cursed, and met in hotel rooms. It was a fast adrenaline rush all the time—with your best friend whom you totally trust. For God's sake, what had I been doing with all that mad public-school organizing and Winnebagos when I could have found all the adventure I was seeking in a single person? Because as I now saw, Mr. Y was love, Mr. Y was life, Mr. Y was magic. He was the elephant in the U-Haul.

• • •

WE FORMED a plan. Although Mr. Y's son was extremely close to both his parents, he was in his last year of art school in the Bay Area, so we told ourselves he was old enough, and he would be fine. My girls, Hannah and Sally, were only six and eight. But they were accustomed to their parents living on separate tracks, often in entirely different cities, so we figured that they, too, would be fine.

All that was left was telling our spouses. Which would be okay because they didn't even like us anymore, we told ourselves. When you looked a bit more carefully, you could see evidence of our spouses' disinterest littered everywhere. Our spouses seemed to prefer traveling without us, when they were out of town they wouldn't call, once home they preferred the eerie glow of their favorite cable programs to the apparently tedious drone of our conversation. It would be a mitzvah. No more bottles of our lotions cluttering the bathroom, tons of closet space would open up, they'd have all that room in the bed to flop around in, better for your back—.

But, of course, humans are humans. What were we thinking?

Kicked out of our homes in scenes alternately gothic and grim, we fled to a cramped 750-square-foot rental unit that, due to a hidden back driveway, with gallows humor Mr. Y dubbed "Pirate's Cove." Our married friends watched in fascination and horror as Mr. Y and I cobbled together a makeshift home, with rust-spotted beach towels and a claw-foot tub piled with 1980s suit jackets and a constantly deflating AeroBed and lone spatulas bought at Target ("And a step stool—to change the lightbulb I think we need a step stool. Also a lightbulb.").

The suffering of our families was far beyond what we'd imagined. We had not anticipated the stunned bewilderment of our parents and parents-in-law, the tearing up of old photos, the racked crying at the kitchen table at midnight. After expressing his shock and pain, Mr. X communicated only through his lawyer, on order to divide our assets and get the divorce done. A shock-black-haired rock-and-roller not known for his shyness, Mr. Y's son swore he would never speak to Mr. Y again. Mr. Y's wife threatened to burn all his clothes and destroy all his things and was having a breakdown. Mr. Y got a call from his mother-in-law, who had rushed to town to be there for her daughter.

Mr. Y finally cracks. I saw it coming because he'd begun spending a lot of time on the darkened porch, pacing and smoking and furtively texting. He looks out of his mind and exhausted—in the last eight months we'd each aged ten years. Sitting at our wobbly two-person dining table, Mr. Y informs me, like a wax figure of his former self, that the madness must stop. If he breaks off all contact and acknowledges his mistake, his wife will allow him to move back home, where his family will close ranks. There he can fulfill his heart's dream—no longer to wander the earth as one of the damned, to be a good father and husband, again to sleep in peace.

Which brings me to why I'm hoisting things into a U-Haul. Mr. Y is moving back home, which is why he's not here to help me with my truck and boxes. By nightfall my beloved will have disappeared back into the bosom of his family, and I'll be thoroughly alone in the mess that I've made of my life. I will be alone in a silent dark rental unit (we have no TV, even) with a teakettle, microwave, and smoking meteorite crater where he and his coats and ties and boots used to be.

Here I stand on a cannonball-torn pirate ship for one, with a destroyed family, a storm fleet of alienated family friends, professional colleagues who are aghast and embarrassed for me, a bunch of pinwheel-eyed public-school-mom friends who are now all themselves scattered in chaos, their gunboats shattered, as I stagger, fatally wounded, toward fifty. I have children, little girls, who were my heart and soul and earth's delight before all this madness. What of my babies? What have I done? Oh God, I say to myself, as I weep at U-Haul, flinging the *Iliad*, the *Odyssey*, and then the *Aeneid* into the Dumpster—*clang, clang, clang.*

I feel in my bones not just the senseless waste of my life, all the good things taken for granted that I have squandered, but the exact measure and weight of my sorrow—and the sorrow of everyone else—as I hurl. Book after book pounds into the Dumpster, bringing perpetual motion but no relief. My heart is broken, my world is dead, my home destroyed. I'm staring into the void. It's the pointless void I have carved out myself, maiming all my loved ones in the process.

It's like waking up the star of one of those Hangover movies. Except that you are not a guy, you are not in your twenties, you have no madcap party buddies, and this is not hilarious.

Bridges

I N T H E M O N T H S A F T E R Mr. Y moved back home to his
family, I trudged on with the horrific business of being a
deeply compromised mother to my wary children and faxing
divorce papers back and forth with Mr. X.

I was having a hellacious time. My life was all upside-down
Tarot cards of jagged weeping during the day and duct-taping
my cell phone shut at night. I attended weird divorced-people
pool parties where at first all these other divorced forty-
somethings seemed amazingly attractive, together and datable
(where have we all been?) and then, as though on Pinocchio's
Pleasure Island, as night fell everyone sprouted donkey ears
and began braying horrible things about being lonely and
angry and desperate (and also fat, we "singles" were all forty-
something and fat now). To combat the chronic sleeplessness
which descended within my four suffocating walls every night
I'd gotten a prescription for Ambien, which due to sleeping
wrong resulted in a temporary paralysis of my right side, making my right arm a limp useless claw. I had tried to fill out

a form for my new very own (I had always depended on my husband's) Ralph's grocery store card with this claw, I had tried to write checks for my daughters' pediatrician with this claw, I had even put in an offer on the perfect Craftsman bungalow that I knew would solve my life with this claw, and had attempted to write the notoriously finicky shy seller a note: "I am a writer and I will take good care of your beautiful home!" But the note ended up looking like something written by a serial killer—it literally read: "I a*& a WME@#$ and I @#! Bdeathmurder home YOU!" I didn't get the house.

I couldn't do anything right. I was devastated, humiliated, and grieving. In the darkness, alone in my squalid apartment, I'd shake my fist into the radio silence of Mr. Y, who was across town, safe in his marital bed, tangled in his wife's 500-thread-count percale sheets.

I knew that my misery was utterly deserved. Lying alone, stricken in this darkened cabin, as I'd abandoned my husband and Mr. Y his wife, now I in turn was abandoned. What idiots we'd been, Mr. Y and I. We had torpedoed our families and children for a love that hadn't stuck.

I BEGAN drinking with a divorced girlfriend named Elise. White wine does not go down well when you're angry— probably red wine or whiskey are better—but chardonnay is what one drank at this ridiculous Westside bistro Elise loved, and I was desperate for company. Men were not Elise's favorite species, so she was drawn to my story like a moth to flame. "I can't believe he would do that to you!" she wailed operatically, clutching my hands in hers. "How could he hurt you like this? What an asshole. Oh Sandra, I'm so sorry."

And while I appreciated the support, I didn't entirely agree. The image she had of me as the jilted middle-aged woman— the victim—was not helpful or entirely accurate. I knew that Mr. Y's decision to move home to his family had been hard. I knew that his wife was a gracious and elegant person, and I knew that Mr. Y's betrayal had been awful for her. I had been irresponsible and narcissistic, destroying his family as well as my own.

"Well, look, Elise," I said. "It's not like my husband left me for a younger woman. I chose to have a damn affair with my best friend of ten years, and he moved home to save his family. It's kind of noble. Kind of beautiful. It's actually what a decent man would do. And I can still have a life. I mean, look at *The Bridges of Madison County*! Two middle-aged people have an affair; Meryl Streep's character makes the honorable decision to preserve her family, and Clint Eastwood's character says, nobly, "Fine, I respect that." He continues to travel the world and have adventures and do cool photography for *National Geographic* and is a romantic cowboy figure. Why shouldn't I be like Clint Eastwood?" I exclaimed, waving an oily bruschetta.

Never mind that Mr. Y and I had had no such noble conversation, and to my knowledge Clint Eastwood never called Meryl Streep in the middle of the night and screamed: "*Why have you done this to me???*" Which is one of the reasons I had started duct-taping my phone shut at night and locking it into my trunk.

Being out on my own (also, giving up drinking, and perhaps moving to an ashram in India) probably would have been a good idea, but, of course, that's not the way it went.

In fact Mr. Y didn't end up at home for very long. In the end the betrayal had been too enormous. After a few months of the marriage's mutually painful continuation, it was his wife who decided they were done. The moral truth is that adulterers deserve being punished—of course we do—but the deeper reality is that middle-aged people like Mr. Y and me are statistically lucky to find anyone who actually really enjoys spending time with us. Which is to say within a year Mr. Y's marriage was finally really over, and he and I were living together again. This time it stuck, and I consider us both to be unfairly blessed.

SINCE OUR reunion Mr. Y and I have begun in bits and pieces to set up a new home together. We've developed a new normal. After the divorce, Mr. X and I established a flexible fifty-fifty custody schedule that worked pretty well (it fluidly accommodated our work, in a similar way as our married, separate-track, co-parenting had). Due to a savagely depressed real estate market and the fact that Mr. X and I both worked a lot during our marriage and were conservative savers, I was able to take my half of the money and buy a three-story Victorian house in Pasadena. While my girls complained about going back and forth between two homes that are twenty miles apart, they also admitted to enjoying our new home's antique pull-down attic and the fact that they had their own bedrooms.

At first Hannah and Sally were understandably wary of Mr. Y, whom they'd known for years as my business partner. But after many fits and starts, my girls eventually got wise to the fact that Mr. Y genuinely likes children, is interested in their tales, never misses a birthday, is generous with ice cream and chocolate, and is one of the few people they can depend on who will always cheerfully buy tons of the crap they're selling for school. While she won't outwardly acknowledge it, this is a huge deal for Sally, who loves school contests the way I once loved refinancing.

Mr. Y's family is not happy that we're together, but they are no longer "in emergency." Time has passed. His ex-wife has a new boyfriend. I write a recommendation for his son to get into an MFA program in Northern California.

Mr. Y and I now have a surprisingly quotidian life. In between writing and teaching and speeches and travel we enjoy such harmless midlife pleasures as flea-market browsing, making salads with carefully toasted pine nuts, and fighting over the only pair of reading glasses in the house. We host dinner parties where our theater friends drink wine and discuss their fascinating projects over the croonings of Chet Baker. Such parties would have been hell for teetotaler Mr. X, who had long ago lost patience for certain kinds of euphoric monologues brayed loudly into the night. But not us. There's always time to talk. What with all of the standing around in the kitchen and gossiping and waving wineglasses, except in the morning, when we are waving coffee mugs, you could well call our home Club Blab. So it appears, in fact, that the giant tear in the cosmic curtain has been finally, mostly, sewed up: that is, until my menopausal freeway hamster meltdown.

Menopause, Old

WHEN I START PONDERING the grand new adventure I'm on called menopause, I get to thinking about my mother. Was this part of what was going on with her? I was eleven when my mother was the age I am today, and that was when things started to go, well, weird. The cause of her change in character was, of course, I now realize, menopause.

But it's also important to note that my mother lived a very different life from the one I do.

Consider, as a twenty-first-century working-mom artifact, my poor twelve-year-old 140,000-mile Volvo. Every morning to my fake surprise I spill an entire travel mug of coffee (with milk) over the gearshift; there are crushed plastic water bottles on the floor amid nests of children's socks (at this point I can't say for sure whose children's; one time I found a boy's tiny Spider-Man underpants in my car—this was weird, as I have only daughters); for an embarrassingly long period of time my car had ants. This is an automotive affliction I've never heard of: I believe it is akin to saying your car has mosquitoes, mice, its own climate zone, or a small problem with gators. The ants were finally traced to a two-and-a-half-year-old banana that my horrified daughters and I discovered in the trunk. We knew the exact age of the banana because it was in a beach bag that had been packed for a specific Fourth of July trip along with a then-new copy of Jonathan Franzen's *The Corrections*. "*The Corrections*! *There* it is!" I exclaimed. So many of the Volvo's dashboard lights are on, each trying to alert me to one malfunction or another, that turning the ignition key is akin to plugging in that big Christmas tree at Rockefeller Center. Yet despite its grievances the car continues—reluctantly—to run (indicating, possibly, that my Volvo is also in menopause). I've been known to drive this ecosystem while wearing a fanny pack and, I regret to say, Crocs.

THE STATE of my Volvo—not to mention Crocs—would have been unthinkable in my mother's world. Hers was the orange-sherbet dreamscape that was Southern California in the 1960s, a stylish Mad Women (instead of Mad Men) era when just going out to the grocery store in one's shiny Buick with tail fins required lipstick and heels. My mother was a five-foot-eleven Valkyrie who wore an apron in the kitchen, a white pleated skirt on the tennis court, and a shiny Pucci-like dress and heavy amber jewelry to visit the butcher (one had those then). The butcher was short and bespectacled but surprisingly tomcat-like as he patrolled his counter, across which they would flirt lightly over roasts and briskets. Oh, the harmless amusements of housewives who didn't make their own money (and hence could not leave the husbands to whom they were unhappily married, as was the case)! The only other personal treat my mother seemed to allow herself was relaxing alone at the far edge of the yard in the falling darkness of the evening, sucking with ferocious meditation on a single Camel cigarette.

It isn't just the Volvo. Motherhood itself is also different than it was fifty years ago. Consider that today not only is no smoking or drinking allowed during pregnancy, there is no red meat, no sushi, and even —according to the husband of a friend of mine—"No smoked fish due to possible secondhand smoke!" My sisters and I were allowed to eat only kale, while stretching headphones playing Mozart over our bellies. At one point I went to pregnancy yoga classes, where I was instructed to go on all fours and waggle my butt in the air to "turn the baby" (positioned for back labor).

I'm a little envious of my mom's Mad Women era, where expectant mothers smoked, drank, and even did amphetamines prescribed to them by their chain-smoking doctors so they wouldn't gain more than twelve pounds in nine months. During labor, the mothers were knocked out so the doctors could pull the babies out with forceps. The dads were sequestered in the waiting room (no amateur videotaping for them), or, even better, they were out and about in colorful madras pants, golfing. On returning home, the babies were cheerfully fed formula by baby nurses. "Oh yeah, we all had baby nurses," my elderly neighbor, Mildred, told me breezily the other day, while waving a Tom Collins in a highball glass. The hiring of baby nurses—no one thought twice about it. It was a regular middle-class occurrence. Recently I read, too, that in imperial

China, aristocratic women had not just baby nurses but wet nurses. This came standard!

The world is better here and now, of course, in many ways, than it was in imperial China, or in the delightfully wicked prefeminist landscape that was the 1960s Americans suburbs. But why, I submit to you, can't we have baby nurses—or wet nurses! Today, women mother while pursuing full-time careers, and pumping our own breast milk in the office. Why, I ask you, can't at least the top 5 percent of executive women—women "leaning in" to high government positions or running *Vogue*, for instance—hire a wet nurse? Why can't it be socially accept-able for these working warriors to chuckle richly when asked how it is that they manage to have it all, responding, "How do I 'have it all'? With my great husband, great housekeeper, great cook, and of course Sierrah. She's getting a BA in art at Sarah Lawrence, minoring in political philosophy, and to earn her way through college she's my wet nurse!"

Just as their fashions, car upkeep, and mothering hab-its were different from ours, so the Mad Women's approach to menopause differed as well. My mother's generation never talked about menopause. We children of menopausal women witnessed only a sudden cataclysmic shift. For ten years, Mom has been standing cheerfully in her yellow apron in the kitchen, drying the dishes. Suddenly, overnight, she is hurling them.

Everyone has stories about how their prefeminist moms or grandmothers or aunts suddenly transformed during the change. (Said one still-changing grandma to me recently: "If anyone tells you menopause is easy? Just *punch them in the mouth*.") Everyone seems to remember the exact moment it happened, and everyone remembers what the ladies threw: Certain contemporaries of mine have separately reported witnessing their menopausal mothers throwing a telephone at the wall, volume M of the *Encyclopædia Britannica* at the cat, and beef Wellington through plate glass.

When I look at this list, one thing strikes me: How deeply cathartic it must have been to hurl an object that actually had heft! And we're talking that certain midcentury heft. Remember those old black dial phones, with the cord? That's something you could really *kachunk*. (Who throws an iPhone? It's just too expensive and actually too light. Where is the payoff? Who throws an iPad? Also frightfully expensive, and it's all backed up in the Cloud anyway. Who throws a Kindle? Why on earth would you throw a Kindle? *Please*.)

Further, regarding beef Wellington, think through for a moment how you'd actually have to prepare it first, which I think involves something en croute in a madeira sauce, not to mention the usual trip with high heels and full makeup to the butcher. How much more satisfying it would have been to hurl through plate glass the meat-and-potatoes-on-platter-style dinners of yore—your whole turkey, your whole spiral-cut ham, your brisket. Who throws a Lean Cuisine? Where is the grandness? I can't throw Make Your Own Pizza at my kids—I would be throwing these . . . sticky strands of . . . ropy dough.

In my family I would trace the change to my mother's forty-ninth birthday. I remember how proudly Kaitlin and I had banded together to give her a birthday present. Clearly, colorful clothes and scarves and jewelry she already had plenty enough of—good Lord, if you looked in her closet (which I did frequently), my mom had at least ten purses that matched her fifty dresses and seventy belts and God knows how many shoes. What we came up with instead was a rectangular glass Pyrex baking dish because we knew how much she loved to bake, and the old metal one was rusty.

Imagine our shock when, for no apparent reason, she screamed and hurled the Pyrex dish against the wall. Then, as with many subsequent episodes, she disappeared into her bedroom like a tide washing out—curtains drawn, door locked. How infuriating it must be when—miserable, wildly hormonally imbalanced—one receives a gift from the children one is tired of endlessly caring and baking for that testifies only to one's further caring and baking for them!

Look: I just want to reiterate that I consider my mom to have done an outstanding job as a mother and wife. She clothed us, fed us, bathed us, made our beds (oh yes), did the laundry, cleaned the house, drove us to all those middle-class suburban lessons, provided a loving ear and shoulder to cry on, and kept all the dental appointments. In the trunk of her gleaming Buick, to keep our strength up, instead of ants, she often had carefully foil-wrapped home-baked cheesecakes, both plain (my favorite) and blueberry (Kaitlin's). She did all this mothering uncomplainingly, in a context of zero career fulfillment (her copious letters suggest she might have enjoyed being a writer) and a marriage only barely made possible not just by her evening Camel cigarette but by the fact that she and my dad slept at opposite ends of the house, an arrangement I grew up thinking was normal. Like the Queen of England or Jackie O, my mom was a class act all the way. In no way do I begrudge her the odd Pyrex toss. All that said, I could never toss a glass Pyrex—or anything else—at, or even in response to, my daughters. I couldn't explode like that at my children because I am way too worried about damaging their feelings of security (which fuel their self-esteem and creativity). Oh no: In this modern era of no parental boundaries, my girls and I are best friends and we talk and talk and talk. Much of it is in the car as sometimes with their commute and schedules we spend as many as three hours a day on the road. (Statistics suggest that today's full-time working mothers spend more hours with their children per week than did 1950s stay-at-homes. I wonder if much of this time is spent in the car, shepherding them to and from activities.) My children can sense how I am feeling by a mere squaring or slump of the shoulders (which they can detect from the backseat while we're flying down the freeway). If I'm tense they'll start massaging my shoulders, and later they may even make me elaborate get-well cards out of colored paper. Never mind that it is colored paper I have actually bought for a work project. No worries, they are completely confident that they will be appreciated for their creativity and sensitivity. There is no shock, there is no awe, there are no boundaries—there is only warm NPR-filler acoustic guitar.

Parenting has changed since the 1960s, and that means that menopause has changed. Today, we so-called helicopter parents worry endlessly about our children's feelings and budding psychological and intellectual development. We do not throw their gifts at the wall, even when said gifts are thoughtless testaments to a lifetime of my baking for them. I *don't* bake for them.

The bad news that follows is: We are not allowed to have gothic moods in menopause, any more than we were allowed to have cigarettes and martinis during pregnancy. I will have to manage my menopause without simply hurling things. I will have to discover some more humane, modern, and enlightened methods. The good news, of course, is that, unlike my mother, I can actually *talk* about the changes age has wreaked upon my body. I can talk to my partner and my caring, outspoken children. I can talk to other women. I can, in fact, write an entire book. What can go wrong?

Menopause, New

I DECIDE TO BEGIN MY journey of exploration by seeing *Menopause: The Musical!* at Mildred's recommendation. This musical will, I learn, soon have enjoyed a longer run even than *Cats*. Mr. Y gallantly offers to accompany me, as is his wont with any theatrical event, but I say: "I don't know, honey. The contrast between our Burning Man romance two years ago and us now attending a Wednesday matinee on menopause seems just a bit sad. I will see you after." So I go by myself.

THE CROWD is, unfortunately, not one I feel particularly at home in. When I arrive thirty minutes before showtime, giant Lincolns and Oldsmobiles are already fishtailing into the jammed parking lot. From behind each car you can see wrinkled bird arms gripping the steering wheel on both sides of a giant head of Barbara Bush hair. *Menopause*'s production values seem *Mr. Toad's Wild Ride*–cheap, the plot negligible (it's about four women bra shopping at Bloomingdale's—I think), the "script" nothing more than parodies of pop hits from the fifties and sixties, rewritten in the vernacular of shvitzing and bloating (instead of the Supremes' "My Guy," think "My Thighs!"). As if possessed by demonic spirits behind my control, of course, I laugh until I cry. I cry as hard or harder than I did that day I pulled off the freeway on my way to Trader Joe's.

I find myself thinking: Is this going to be me? South Florida retirement home? Barbara Bush hair? Mustaches and bifocals? Cats and crocheting? Is this the passage I'm entering now?

Stopping off for some emergency wine on the way home, I salve my wounds with a perusal of *Vanity Fair*, which always lends my grocery shopping some much-needed glamour. Slowly turning pages in the checkout line, I find myself becoming fascinated with a piece about Courtney Love, sojourning at the time in Britain. It is startling enough to consider Love's "retirement" scheme, which seemed to encompass three main activities: drinking Pimm's Cups, attending foxhunts, and hoping to marry somewhere, somehow, into the British nobility. Even more startling for me, though, is the revelation that the mood-swingy mother of Francis Bean Cobain will soon turn fifty. I feel better already.

Oh my God, I think. See! This will be different! This country has aged so much even that Gen Xers are going through the change, and it's not going to be the same for us. There won't be Barbara Bush haircuts and Oldsmobiles. I understand in a moment of inspiration that my generation will by necessity be part of the new menopause. Ours will be as different from the old menopause as a white pleated tennis skirt is from Crocs. Or some other better, younger, hipper fashion statement. This is our time! Ready, set, *menopalooza*!

This will be huge. Subsequent research confirms just how huge. Whereas in 1900, due to an average life span of forty-eight years, many females never really reached menopause, today women between the ages of forty-four and sixty-five have become America's largest demographic group. Think of it: We are literally the largest swarm of menopausal women in history. Picture fifty million Courtney Loves running around this country making a very giant Hole, and not just in the ozone layer. By 2015 nearly one-half of American women will be menopausal.

Good Lord, I think, this is not going to be some sideline event. Think of the celebrities alone who are menopausal or post: Madonna, Demi Moore, Oprah, Suze Orman, Katie Couric, Kathie Lee Gifford. Or politicians: possible future president Hillary Clinton, Sarah Palin (who shares my birthday, February 11), and German chancellor, Angela Merkel. *Fortune* magazine recently ran a cover story on the world's one hundred most powerful women—90 percent of them are, their ages suggest, menopausal. Forget the old menopause's image of your lovable mustached, gray-haired aunt Edna in a shower cap, saying, "Oy, I'm shvitzing," or "Where are my glasses?" (Children in petticoats gaily shout back: "They're on top of your head!") In the new menopause, these steely-eyed women are driving the freeways, running businesses, doing newscasts, setting interest rates, performing dental surgery.

Furthermore, even when one takes a look at the women in

one's own day-to-day life, one may have no idea who's going through the change. At least in my hometown of Los Angeles, many of these ladies do not look fifty. What with the Botox, the Restylane, the Pilates, the low lights, and God knows what else, a menopausal woman may look like a thirty-four-year-old with incredible Pilates arms who hasn't slept in a year and will tear your head off in the checkout line because she has not had a carb since 1997.

I start to suspect, given the vastness and edginess of the demographic, that there must be a bunch of hip, great new books on menopause. Surely my enlightened "younger" generation has developed a strategy for getting this thing done in a new, enlightened way. What does Oprah have to say about it? I wonder. Suze Orman? *Real Simple*? Invigorated by the positive forward momentum of my research project, I go to my local bookstore. I make my way to the Women's Health and Self-Help sections and, behind a life-size cutout of Dr. Phil, there is indeed an avalanche of menopause titles. Eagerly I place as many as will fit into my basket. These include: *Could It Be . . . Perimenopause?*; *Before Your Time: The Early Menopause Survival Guide*; *The Natural Menopause Plan*; *Second Spring*; *Menopause Reset!: Reverse Weight Gain, Speed Fat Loss*; *Get Your Body Back in 3 Simple Steps*; and the slightly ominously titled *What Nurses Know . . . Menopause* (two words: *atrophic vaginitis*). These menopause books link to more menopause books, which I troll on Amazon.com.

After a couple of weeks of reading I start seeing some patterns.

On the cover of a typical menopause book, instead of the

fanged woman with the spiky Medusa-do one might expect, one is far more likely to see a lone flower—a poppy, or perhaps a daisy. This type of wan little affirmation symbol actually fits, because the war stories of the MD, PhD, and RN authors who dominate this genre contain narratives that are indeed kind of, well, Stuart Smalley–esque. Here's a pastiche:

> Mary Anne, age forty-eight, came into my office feeling overweight and bloated. She hadn't been sleeping, work was stressful, her husband had just gone on disability, and he required daily care. Mary Anne complained to me of lower-back problems and gastritis, and also cramping during sex, which had become more and more infrequent. She was extremely depressed about moving her eighty-four-year-old mother to a nursing home, and upon examination I noticed vaginal inflammation.

Yikes! As unappetizing as that just was to read, be glad you saw only one such passage—I must have read a hundred. Because clearly, from the medical-professional point of view, menopause, along with the ungainly run-up to it called perimenopause—which appears to be the phase that I am in now—is a parade of baleful, bloated middle-aged women ("Lisa, fifty-two," "Carolyn, forty-seven," "Suzanne, sixty-one") trudging into their doctors' offices complaining of lower-back pain and family caregiving issues and diminished libidos and personal dryness and corns. As they sit wanly on cold metal tables in their paper gowns, they arduously count out their irregular periods—from thirty-five days to forty-four days to fifty-seven, going heavy to light, light to heavy, sometimes with spotting, sometimes with flooding, sometimes flood-spotting, sometimes spot-flooding. Our symptoms are various. They include mood swings, sudden weight gain, and the appearance of morning chin hairs that by noon are long enough to braid and twirl up into thick Princess Leia buns.

AND SO, for these new, hip, bloated, and only perhaps sometimes frumpy Gen Xers—menopausal, yes, but in the throes of careers, raising children, caring for our elders, and . . . let me start the conversation. Let me lead you quickly and relatively painlessly through the science of your symptoms, or symptoms to come. The fact is, few perimenopausal women have the time, inclination, or stamina to wade through hundreds of pages of Eeyore stories, hormonal bar graphs, and endless treatises on vitamins and omega-3. We need our facts fast, concise, and perhaps on a key chain or zip card, the back of which can be used to quickly swipe for groceries, which may well include a coupon for emergency chocolate or wine, just because it's Wednesday. We have a child to pick up in an hour whose fourth-grade global environment project will require not just frantic Googling but faux, wide-eyed active listening—hurling the whole (Styrofoam) thing out the window is apparently not an option. So, trek shoes on, water bottles up: Let's do this thing. Herewith, as a public service for my suffering sisters in the new menopause, is a simple, handy menopause one-sheet and walk-through of the science.

HANDY MENOPAUSE ONE-SHEET

*(for Perimenopausal Women with
Frighteningly Short Attention Spans)*

TYPICAL PERIMENOPAUSE SYMPTOMS

Irregular periods

Hot flashes

Night sweats

Vaginal dryness

Breast tenderness

Drop in libido

Bloating

Weight gain around the belly

Forgetting things/inability to concentrate

Heart palpitations

Sleeplessness

Mood swings

Depression

Panic

Anxiety

Sometimes all at the same time

Of course many women may read this list and wonder: Except for the hot flashes, how is this so terribly different than my life before menopause?

QUICK EXPLANATION OF THE SCIENCE

(for Perimenopausal Women Sadly Lacking a PhD in Biology)

Perimenopause is a somewhat loosey-goosey term for the period before menopause, when your periods become less regular, which can happen as early as your late thirties or early forties (and can supposedly last from four to fifteen years!). A common rule of thumb is about forty-six.

What's going on hormonally? Deep breath. During the first part of a twenty-eight-day cycle, follicles in your ovaries make estrogen. During the second part, progesterone surges to make the uterine lining ready for the fertilized egg.

But now, if you start *not* making an egg, your body stops making progesterone and your "unopposed estrogen" rises, resulting in many lovely perimenopausal symptoms. Eventually your estrogen levels will also drop, so your relative balances of estrogen and progesterone may start fluctuating wildly.

But listen: Note that there's a complex relationship between these hormones and the workings of your actual brain! That's a simplified way of saying that this whole fertility conversation is taking place among a rogues' gallery of potentially misbehaving body parts. A short list includes the hypothalamus, the pituitary gland, the ovaries, body fat, GnRH (gonadotropin-releasing hormone), FSH (follicle-stimulating hormone), the brain's temporal lobe and limbic areas (which regulate our moods), and the brain's amygdala and hippocampus (related to memory, hunger, libido, and anger—let the party begin!).

Menopause (defined as a full year without any periods) is what comes after.

In *The Silent Passage*, Gail Sheehy's celebrated book on menopause, she calls it "the calm after the storm." Weirdly, menopausal women's hormone levels now become not just stable but in fact the same as preadolescent girls'. Menopausal women also have not just the same amount of (free) testosterone they had in fertility—sometimes they have more! (Which may suggest I'll grow a mustache and shout more when driving, but I'll cross that bridge when I come to it!)

WHAT ON EARTH TO DO ABOUT IT

There was an infamous and popular (isn't there always?) 1966 book called *Feminine Forever*, by Robert Wilson, MD. Being of the "menopause as crepey dethroned queen" school, Wilson urged women to take estrogen pills to keep themselves youthful and moist and sexy. As a result, lots of menopausal women started taking a product called Premarin. Literally made from horse urine, Premarin also seemed to have the unfortunate side effect of potentially causing breast cancer, heart attacks, blood clots, and more. (This bombshell came in a 2002 Women's Health Initiative study that had followed 160,000 women over twenty years.)

When the news came out everyone freaked, and the conventional wisdom became *no* hormones.

Now, however, the pendulum is swinging back to center. Some HRT (hormone replacement therapy), for a limited amount of time, is considered safe. As opposed to horse urine, what seems to be in vogue now are "bioidenticals," largely thanks to Suzanne Somers's long-term enthusiastic endorsement of same. Bioidenticals match the hormones already in your body, although they are made from plants. While that seems more "organic," some doctors caution that there are no long-term studies that demonstrate the safety of bioidenticals, and some even consider compounding pharmacies a kind of medical voodoo world. As my wonderful gynecologist says, "Suzanne Somers giving medical advice is as if I bought a mutual fund and said, Let me give you financial advice." She believes straight Premarin is fine (not the Prem-pro combination that set off the scare in the Women's Health Initiative study). Then, of course, many other people use bioidenticals and love them, with no ill effects.

In the end there is no one magic bullet to alleviate menopausal symptoms, because women are so different. See your doctor. And try not to get a needless hysterectomy.

Some women prefer to alleviate their symptoms without any hormones at all. Typical recommended over-the-counter menopause-symptom-soothing aids include black cohosh tea, Saint-John's-wort, soy, chamomile, calcium, vitamin supplements (D and B-12), and phytoestrogens (plant-based forms of estrogen found in alfalfa sprouts, soybeans, chickpeas, lentils, tofu, miso, flaxseed, and spinach).

In short, the literature on menopause confirms that perimenopause could well be a wild roller coaster of anger, depression, sleeplessness, plunging libido, bloating, and vaginal dryness. How should you deal with all of this? Through (go, team!) a healthy lifestyle! Essentially, the chorus of books all agree: We're to get more exercise, drink more water, do yoga stretches before bed, cut out alcohol and caffeine, and yet (and how does this follow?) reduce stress. Even the flirty exhortations to have more sex feel like yet another job on life's chore wheel (given that it's supposed to be with your mate of twenty years rather than with Johnny Depp in his *Pirates of the Caribbean* garb or Hugh Jackman in any garb at all).

ALL OF which is to say that now, having learned everything there is to know about this wacky hormone dance I've begun, instead of feeling free and elated I feel like I've just been given an odious homework assignment (what with everyone's chipper exhortations to "Just eat more flaxseed! And soy!"). To be candid, I am extremely disappointed that there isn't a magic bullet and that now, as in pregnancy, I am supposed to start doing yoga again and to eat kale. They didn't help at all then, and I hardly believe they will now.

All the medical advice in these books has gotten me down.

I'm very bad at cutting things out.

I would like to bring things back in. I'm an action-oriented gal.

I'm not going to make it through this thing unless there is a completely other way. Otherwise I'll just have to resort to what my mother did at the end of every day: smoking.

Life in the (Happiness) Projects

**THE THINGS WE TRIED IN
OUR JOURNEY TOWARD HAPPINESS**

Singing

Dancing

Sculpting

Crocheting

Giving up Solitaire

(Extreme!) couponing

Exercising

Painting our bedrooms mad different colors like Burnt
    Tangiers

Writing "gratitude" notes to everyone in our lives

If not that, at least buying a bunch of "gratitude"
    stationery

Weeping

Throwing in the towel and just buying ourselves some
    damn colorful plateware

Frantic late-night fressing

Xanax

O F COURSE THE PROBLEM with perimenopause is for-getfulness. When you're in perimenopause—even after you've been told you are—you keep forgetting who you are. I would advise all women who've begun the change to write a note: "REMEMBER! I AM IN PERIMENOPAUSE! THIS COULD TAKE FOUR TO FIFTEEN YEARS!" and stick it on your bathroom mirror so you can see it every morning.

The forgetfulness is why, after I got that first attack of the "darkies" in the car, read all those menopause books, and became disappointed that there was no magic bullet—I totally forget about the whole thing. That's right, I just totally forget about it. All I notice is that I am just sort of depressed. Every morning, I wake up feeling as though something—this name-less weight—is sitting on my chest and neck, gradually pressing the breath out of me. It's less hat full of rain than a kind of handbag, or purse, full of anxiety. My body is also sometimes suffused with sudden tingling, uncomfortable warmth, but it doesn't occur to me at this time to call it anything exciting like a hot flash.

On my parenting days off, when I'm not pounding around town with my kids, I find myself becoming weirdly listless. I have a vague memory that there is something I could take for this, like Saint-John's-wort or black cohosh tea, but I have no idea what black cohosh tea is, and even the notion of get-ting into the car to drive to where some perky health-food-store employee is going to explain it to me (why are health-food

explanations always so *long*?) fills me with exhaustion. In point
of fact, daily activities like "going to the store," "taking a walk,"
or even "getting dressed" have come to seem oddly daunting.
I feel like some lady staring flatly out the window in a Cymbalta commercial—but of course I never make the connection
that *maybe what I actually need is Cymbalta*—whatever that is.
I'm too embarrassed at the end of the day to report to anyone
but Mr. Y (who sees it) how pathetic I've been. What did I
do today? I stayed in bed until noon. I perused a home decor
magazine. I played computer Solitaire. I Q-tipped my ears. The
Q-tipping—that was arguably my happiest moment, as well as
my most productive.

"I think it's because you're not writing some big new project," Mr. Y says. "The magazine articles are one thing. But you'll
feel much better when you get a new book going."

"Do you know how hostile that is?" I flash back, stung.
"Telling a person they'll cheer up if they just get a book going
only makes them feel worse! Coming up with a great creative
project is a hard thing to do, and if one's happiness depends on
that, one should contemplate quitting life entirely. 'Be creative!'
Gee thanks! It's another impossible chore, next to the sink full
of dishes and the basket of laundry."

"Why don't you call Clare," Mr. Y pushes on, "from your
writers' group? She's always got ten things going. You always
seem to stimulate each other."

Not wanting to be accused of ignoring his advice, although
ignoring his advice is exactly my instinct, I call Clare, who is
indeed a beloved sister-in-arms. She is a middle-aged mother of
two who also has three well-reviewed novels to her credit. Like

me, she is doing the mothering/writing balancing act, although on her this always seems a lot more fun.

When I ask her what she's up to, and if she wants to get our group going again, she delivers a grand announcement: "I've given up writing."

"What?" I say.

Clare explains matter-of-factly that over the past few years her books have seemed to sell less and less well, she is not even that excited about writing them anymore, her husband's business is thriving now anyway, she's sick of feeling guilty about not writing, and what she has become interested in instead is the subject of happiness.

Happiness?

"Stop it, Kyle," she says to her son. "Happiness! Yes! I've started to do all this reading, and it's pretty fascinating. For instance, the World Health Organization has done this massive study across five continents. Turns out most affluent nations— not just ours—have higher rates of depression than poorer ones. Isn't that interesting? There's also this *National Geographic* guy named Dan Buettner who's been studying what he calls 'blue zones'—the world's happiest cities and villages. Not only are 'strong social bonds' key to happiness, also key—check this out—is minimizing things you don't enjoy. Top three least favorite activities of all people around the globe? *Ding, ding, ding!* Child care, commuting, and housework!"

"Oh my God," I say, "that's exactly our lives. Or at least 50 percent of mine. So what's my excuse?"

"No, no, no, Kyle!" I hear Clare exclaim. "No! You've had two already! Anyway," she continues, "there's also this thing called 'the paradox of declining female happiness.' This was a Wharton School study where, using thirty-five years of data, economists found in spite of educational and employment advances, women were actually becoming less happy rather than more."

"That's depressing. So what does one do?"

"Well, of course you can change your point of view. I looked at one book called *Stumbling on Happiness*. It was all about quieting the mind and letting happiness come to you, but it seemed too Zen."

"Yeah, sure, meditation. No."

"I do better with more of a project," she says. "It's more motivating for me to think of happiness as something I have to hunt down with a club, kill, chop into pieces, and drag home. That's the idea behind this *New York Times* best-selling book called *The Happiness Project*. Not the chopping and killing part, but where you literally make happiness into a project. The author, Gretchen Rubin, says that there are plenty of us moms who have good jobs and healthy kids and supportive partners but we still feel this sort of malaise. Phew. So it's not just me. She begins the memoir sitting on a bus, looking out a rain-splattered window and wondering why her life feels so flat, and when I read that page I said, Bingo, that's my kind of book!"

I'M RELIEVED to hear someone talk about chasing the blues away in such a rigorous proactive way.

Clare and I decide we will both do happiness projects, and

we will apply the same discipline to them as when we were writing books. Which is to say we will meet once a week and hold each other strictly accountable. We are going to strap on trek shoes and fill water bottles and, dammit, we're going to get this happiness thing done.

This morning I am already mightily cheered simply to be sitting on her familiar tan leather couch in her familiar cozy den framed with her familiar light boxes of cheerful garden windows. I like her kids well enough, but I couldn't be more glad they're at school right now.

This is great. This is great.

Just the act of smartly pulling out matching yellow legal pads is a reassuring Pavlovian exercise. Tearing off the plastic is a restorative act. Pilot pens are out, herbal tea mugs are filled, and it feels like our lives, like rivers, are coursing forward.

Clare puts on her glasses and begins reading: "A 'happiness project' is an approach to changing your life. First is the preparation stage, when you identify what brings you joy, satisfaction, and engagement, and also what brings you guilt, anger, boredom, and remorse." Clare looks at me. "Guilt, anger, boredom, remorse. What brings them?"

"Ugh," I sigh. "What doesn't?" The truth is, I feel so shaky these days anything can tip me over.

"Well, of course," I admit, "there are the usual quotidian irritants that can suddenly cause the elevator to drop. The overflowing laundry basket, this recent bill for two thousand dollars in back taxes I just got from the IRS, the continual both urgent and completely-impossible-to-understand-in-way-too-tiny-a-font missives from my daughter's schools . . . 'Fund-raising! Jogathon! Gift wrap! Book drive! Book drive for the Jogathon! Jogathon for the book drive! And also bring lemons! Very important that we have the lemons!' *What* lemons?

"More puzzling, though, are those things that aren't by nature sad but that still cause the floor to fall out. For no reason at all."

Clare empathizes, and we decided to call them "gloomlets." However trivial, we make up our lists.

Sandra's Gloomlets

- The sound of the voice of this particular classical music DJ we have here in Los Angeles named Jim Svejde—used to love it; now it fills me with an unutterable suffocating sadness
- My eleven-year-old's wish to become a contortionist for Cirque du Soleil—I fear her dreams will be crushed in the big competitive dog-eat-dog world of . . . contortionism (?)
- The color yellow
- This show on the Food Network called *Pioneer Woman*
- I really don't have any great shoes, and this absolutely frustrates me
- All manner of muffins (aka can't have)
- Puppies
- Vivaldi
- Wall calendars from my realtor or from the bank— feels like a used-car salesman actually drove a 2007 Ford Fiesta with a sagging muffler over my grave

- The food samples at Trader Joe's—so limited, always so disappointing
- The color yellow—did I say that already? The color yellow? I have no attention span

Clare's Gloomlets (and "I don't know why I'm overidentifying with the downward arcs of celebrities, but . . .")

- The fact that Dr. Phil is just not as amazing as he once was—now his show just seems kind of trashy
- Speaking of which, the fall of Oprah; thought she was invincible—she keeps putting it out there, but can't escape the fact that golden age is gone
- Cilantro
- Smell of cilantro
- Spelling of the word "cilantro"
- The kind of Lean Cuisine that has only pasta and vegetables
- The fact that cake pops are so tiny and yet they are 170 calories each

I am curious as to how depressed Clare has actually been, since experiencing the writer's block and hopelessness around her latest book.

"Oh my God," she says. "The massive night eating, the drinking—Scotch, why am I now suddenly drinking Scotch?—and weirdly enough, it sounds strange, but—"

"But what?"

"Computer Solitaire."

Oh well. I assured her that everyone does that.

"But I mean it's bad," she says. "Some days I will play so much my fingers ache. I'm saying literally so much I will look up at the clock, see two hours have vanished, and I'll be so depressed by the gigantic waste of time I'll immediately think about having some Valium. This is before ten in the morning."

"Well, look," I say. "Even Jonathan Franzen has admitted to a Solitaire fetish. Presumably his close friend David Foster Wallace did not have a Solitaire fetish, but sadly look how that turned out. Perhaps, in fact, Solitaire is the only thing keeping us going. Perhaps being addicted to Solitaire puts us into a kind of emotionally healthy Jonathan Franzen camp, as opposed to a not-able-to-experience-pleasure-at-all David Foster Wallace camp."

So I manage to convert even that into a win. What can I say? We are flailing. We are taking this happiness thing one day at a time.

"Anyway—good—great," Clare says, tearing her list off her tablet. "Gretchen Rubin says that's just the first half of the process. The second is, and I quote, 'the making of resolutions, when you identify the concrete actions that will boost your happiness.' As evidenced by Rubin's subtitle: *Why I Spent a Year Trying to Sing in the Morning, Clean My Closets, Fight Right, Read Aristotle, and Generally Have More Fun.*"

"Fun," I wonder aloud. "Yes. Whatever happened to fun?"

"At one time, if I recall, you had yourself a bit too much of it."

"That is true."

"But here's the thing." Clare leans forward, her voice dropping. "Outside of a rip-roaring affair, which you had, and which was fun for a moment before it became absolutely horrible, have you ever noticed how often the adult things that are supposed to be 'fun' really aren't? Adult 'mixers,' for instance. Don't you dread them? Or the beach. Yikes!"

"Or certain holidays."

"Or holidays on the beach. Like Fourth of July."

"The worst."

"The parking, the shlepping, the Gladware."

"The fireworks' too-loud booms and the sand in the undies and the hysterical exhausted children."

"Farmer's markets," she says. "On what planet is that a fun weekend activity? Alan—" her long-suffering husband "—took us to one the other week. First I always think: We're going to the fair, the fair, the fair! But then I always find, on approach to those tents—those sort of self-satisfied, pointy little blue tents—I actually feel dread. Dread! Why? Because it's the Lucy-and-the-football thing over and over again. I always look eagerly toward the first line of booths as though I'm going to see something Willy Wonka wonderful, but oh no, it's just piles of bok choy. Bok choy and turnip greens and broccolini, the very things I try to avoid at restaurants. There is too much organic produce. Why am I pawing through all this produce?"

"Well, it is a farmer's market," I say. "It's what farmers sell."

"Sure," she says. "I get that now. But as I've found, the high point of farmer's markets has nothing to do with farmers. The high point is the Julia Child moment—"

"Oh no, not even the Julia Child moment but the Meryl Streep playing Julia Child moment—"

"Oh no—next level," she says "The Meryl Streep playing

Julia Child in a Nora Ephron movie moment, when you select some artisanal vegetable that will be part of some amazing transformative dish you're actually never planning to cook. Three weeks later, as usual, you're pitching all those weeping brown legumes into the garbage. Summer squash? Mustard greens? Organic heirloom Japanese tomatillos? Why do I want these? Why would anyone? Who have I become?"

"Exactly," I say.

"What about Kickstarter?" she adds, shrilling higher. "Pardon me, but I don't want to hear about anyone else's Kickstarter. The album, the play, the film—why is funding everyone else's creative project suddenly up to me?"

"That's right," I agree. "There used to be another word for Kickstarter. It was called 'grandparents.'"

We embrace the notion of a happiness-boosting field trip, which will involve shopping but—here's the key, we decide— not at any depressing stores.

"I can't face Michael's," I say. "I've been there too many times on emergency scavenger hunts working off fourteen-item lists for my daughters' awful school projects. The fiberboard, the dowels, the button eyes, the glue guns." One of our most notorious escapades was Hannah's fourth-grade "California mission," when, while trying to affix the lopsided bell tower, with a scream I accidentally jammed a toothpick into my thumb, resulting in the project's new moniker: "Mission of Blood."

"No Michael's," Clare agrees, shivering. "I friggin' hate that place. We'll go to the fancy German-named art store we never allow our children to enter because everything costs three times as much."

Seizing the moment, we fill up our water bottles, jump into her Prius, and immediately:

Go to Blau's to buy Clare some clay for sculpting ("I've never sculpted!" she declares, "I want to sculpt!").

Go to the music store to buy sheet music for Clare to learn to sing the entire score of *West Side Story*. Back in the car, she throws her arm up into the air and keens: "One handed catch!"

Go to Crate and Barrel to brainstorm mad new paint colors for my too-ice-blue and hence to-me-depressing bedroom—perhaps a hue called "Burnt Tangiers." I can actually visualize this color in my brain. It echoes a kind of Moroccan burnt tangerine color I once saw in some throw pillows on some wicker in some other section. We also energetically smell—and savor—and enjoy—and meditate on—about fourteen different "flavors" (Rosemary Mint, Japanese Plum, Ylang-Ylang) of six- and twelve-inch pillar candles. *Ommm.*

Go to Cost Plus World Market to buy severely colorful plates. Severely. To "happy up" the chore-filled eyesore that has become my home, I've decided that everything in my household must please the eye. Also a set of four hand-painted coffee mugs. "I need something to get up for in the morning!" I exclaim. "I want a pretty mug! Not just all these dismal chipped unmatched things from all those damn public-radio pledge drives."

On our way to Target (less depressing than CVS) to pick up persimmon-colored (and why not?) nail polish, Clare's eye lands on a *USA Today* magazine. Its cover is a cheery megablast about the joys of "extreme couponing." "Look how happy that woman looks!" Clare marvels. "Why have I never couponed? That sounds like fun. I want to start couponing!" This reminds me of how my mother used to collect Blue Chip stamps in the sixties. I share the memory: "I totally remember my mom sitting at the dining room table in the afternoons gluing those Blue Chip stamps into that neat little booklet—it seemed so deeply pleasurable. That, and her cigarette at the end of the day. In fact, I feel like I have some memory of her blissfully doing Blue Chip stamps while smoking cigarettes." Feeling psyched, we pick up twin green plastic sleevelets that can apparently be used as coupon organizers.

Not to leap ahead here, but before we keep going, pencils up:

MENOPAUSE QUESTION

When it comes to menopause/depression tips, why do typical lists of "solutions" always look like activities one would do at a Finnish Christian work-study camp for moderately slow children? Why is it always:

> Sing!
> Clean out your closets!
> Organize your sock drawer (you'll be amazed at how
>   satisfying it is)!
> Take a daily walk!
> Hydrate, hydrate, hydrate!
> Cut and arrange some fresh flowers in a pretty vase!

Why don't those lists ever have items like:

> Have a pitcher of margaritas and just get fucking
> bombed!
> YouTube until your eyes bleed to see who's fat in a
> bikini!
> Eat raw chocolate-chip cookie dough until you puke!
> How about a heady bit of Nordstrom's shoplifting?!
> Three words: Bang a sailor!

Just asking. "One handed catch!"

I find that, by hook or by claw, my happiness project is actually working. These manic "project" activities masquerading as incredibly happy busy-ness are doing an okay job of covering up some of the day's shifting fogs and fens of stealth guerrilla depression. Perhaps it is because my little projects give me something to focus on, like a cat distracted into hypnotically batting a paw against colorful guppies in a fishbowl, while at the same time being free of anxiety-producing deadlines, negative critiques, or yardsticks of dwindling resources. (For example, I've long enjoyed the tactile, deft, satisfying keyboard-smacking experience of paying my bills with Quicken, and yet no amount of colorful pie charts can mask the fact that month by month my money is draining away.) As I beaver away at my personal not-connected-to-anything-at-all-crucial to-do lists, it is like the first day of school, red apple in hand, snap of autumn, when I was young and first realized: "Yay! I am good at sitting at a desk and filling pages with neat if perhaps not always terribly meaningful handwriting! And I will get rewarded for it!"

I can't really do much about global warming, world hunger, or the deficit. Today's problems are too large, overwhelming, and ever present, on that twenty-four-hour news cycle. You can recycle all year long, but get on a plane and in a flash your eco-footprint sprouts giant bunions. So one's goals begin to shrink. And that passitivity on my part is rather sad. After all, my generation of females came of age in postrevolutionary times: The good fight had been fought, we had coed schools, a pro-choice society, and all avenues of personal freedoms open to us. Our generation of women was going to change the world—to feminize the power structure and workplace while giving up our subjugation at home. So why then, three decades later, are we staring in a glaze into a Starbucks vitrine counting the calories in a raspberry cake pop? It's all we can do to manage our own moods in a day. It's all we can do to watch HGTV until noon and not overdose on antidepressants, and that itself is sad. Because are we not still women? Do we not still roar? Do we perhaps need our own female version of a Fight Club? All big questions and a bit too much to take on, but in the meantime, what's wrong with a little extreme couponing? That's a win-win. Because now I am no longer passive. And I am no longer focused on my usual also Sisyphean tasks. Mortage, what mortgage? Health-insurance premiums, what health-insurance premiums? So what if my IRA has so declined in value that my children will be able to afford only three hours of community college? That's not what's at stake here! My happiness projects have one goal: happiness!

. . .

I AM CONTINUING to build around myself a protective, ever-growing mandala of crisp new legal pads and folders and binders. Ever more ideas and lists and resolutions are coming to me—Pilot pen out:

I'm going to finally, for once in my life, drink eight glasses of water a day and see what actually happens (I buy a metallic blue water bottle—just admiring its sheen makes me happy)!

I'm going to get a sassy new haircut!

I'm going to get a pair of those new Shape-up-type thingies!

One of these days I'm even going to decide what version of Burnt Tangiers I want to go with, as my bedroom walls are covered with so many slightly different paint colors by now it looks like an insane asylum!

In fact, next level, I'm going to actually finally open all those old Pirate's Cove cardboard boxes and rebuild my small personal library. I will perhaps even—oh hey, *ding, ding, ding!*—rebuy *One Hundred Years of Solitude*. I will commit to correcting my youthful past by even reading a South American magical-realist novel all the way through, and maybe at least one Henry James!

This will of course require bookshelves. Mr. X used to take care of things like bookshelves, but I doubt he will do that for me any longer. If I ask Mr. Y to procure shelves, they will be—I don't know—like "stage shelves" (being that Mr. Y is not the handiest person). No matter: I dog-ear pages of the IKEA catalog for bookshelves that the new claw-free me will assemble myself!

I find I am thinking with unusual swiftness and clarity and penetration. My thoughts flow quickly and easily.

I have come up with ideas for three books, four one-woman shows, and a community-based (think Zip Car) Costco purchase-share plan!

I'm going to write a blog about my happiness project, a happiness blog!

I'm going to create a happiness app, a depression app, and a "what the hell is an app" app!

I am labeling all my ideas on color-coded charts in color-coded folders in color-coded files in my brand-new file cabinet. It is one from Staples with 237 individual screws and twenty-seven steps that it took me seven hours to hand-assemble. I am not kidding.

In moving several boxes of books to make way for the cabinet, with the Herculean energy of a crazed lumberjack, I see an old paperback on Southern recipes and hostessing. It is a book outlining what to serve at funerals called *Just Because You're Dead Is No Excuse.* How very true! I laugh. In the mail, intrepid menopause specialist Ann has sent me some catalogs especially targeted for middle-aged women. What fun! With enigmatic names like *As We Change* and *Solutions*, they contain fascinating items like bathing suits with skirts and bathtub reading racks with a wineglass holder and special toe-bunion spreaders. Excitedly I mark my catalog and order up a storm! Sure! *As We Change . . . Solutions*!

CLARE HAS crashed.

She is still in her bathrobe at 11:00 A.M. Her two kids are home with the flu. They are parked on the living room couch, watching Nick 2. The TV wails and wails and wails. Clare's ankle is swollen and wrapped in ice in an Ace bandage. She looks terrible.

"What happened to your foot?" I ask.

She puts her hand up. Her voice is toneless.

"Remember how excited I was about the couponing?"

I nod. It was the one activity I hadn't gotten to.

"So I read the *USA Today* article about it, and it turns out what really gets these couponers going is double couponing, triple couponing, and extreme couponing. It's surprisingly technical. You can't go on impulse. To rack up those savings, you have to be really disciplined.

"So I open up my Sunday paper," she says, "I pull out all those glossy coupon sheets I typically ignore, and I begin cutting them out. I see a coupon for Air Wick, regularly a dollar twenty-nine, today a dollar nineteen. There's a five-cents-off coupon for a two-pack of rubber bands. Next up, six Irish Spring deodorants for five dollars. And instead of feeling excited, I'm starting to feel sort of sick. Rubber bands? Air Wick? I don't even want this stuff. It's depressing!

"And look at this," she says. "I clicked on some wrong savings link, and now I'm starting to get all these strange e-mails. Here's an ad that was sent to me just this morning. It shows— look!—this silver-haired woman who is really really excited about . . . catheter delivery. Who are all these crazy beeyotches? And, oh my God, is this, in just a few short years, going to become me? The thing is that I do adore home delivery, and I can almost, almost imagine how delivery of a personal medical device like a catheter could really provoke some excitement!

But maybe I'm just lashing out desperately and losing my mind! Maybe instead of really happy, all of America's women including me are just really, really insane!

"So I'm now looking around the house," she continues, "and instead of happy I'm feeling kind of pathetic. My kids think my singing is terrible. My sculptures look like frozen poo. I can't even cut coupons without a meltdown—I don't have one-tenth of the coping power of one of those . . . those cat ladies who collect Hummel figurines. I used to mock my mother for doing that, and now instead of mocking her I am amazed by her because she led such a more limited life but seemed much more happy. What I would give to be made happy by a cat and some Hummel figurines—think of all the money I would save! Who wouldn't prefer a cat and Hummel figurines over antidepressants? So yesterday when the kids were at school, I'm sitting in my bathrobe playing Solitaire like some addicted lab rat. Jesus the gardener appears suddenly, like this apparition, just outside my home-office window, with his panama hat, leaf-blowing. I am suddenly frightened that Jesus will look up and see his middle-aged First World lady 'boss' playing Solitaire while Jesus is actually working for a living."

"Sure," I say. Inwardly I coin a phrase: "Soliterror"—the terror that another person is going to come up behind you and see those white cards floating on that telltale green background. Mr. X used to catch me playing Solitaire when he would water plants just outside my office, and he was as outraged as if I were streaming porn. ("You told me and the kids to leave you alone to write, and you're sitting at your desk playing Solitaire!" "I'm just warming up to write!" I'd protest.)

"So before Jesus's hat can tilt up and he sees me," Clare continues, "I try frantically to click over to another screen, away from the cards—but I click and click and click and it isn't switching. Starting to panic, I try to reach behind the computer to actually yank out the power cord. Never mind saving the game, I think . . . it's all lost! It's all lost! Do you see? I actually find myself thinking the words: 'It's all lost.' But alas, as I lunge forward I actually fall off my chair, right onto a now-broken plate—that had also flown off my desk—of a Starbucks cream-cheese-and-apple muffin. I am the first person in history ever to have sprained her ankle playing Solitaire."

"Oh, I'm sure many others have done that," I say unconvincingly.

"I've got to give it up cold turkey. Kyle! Kyle! No!"

"Oh no," I say. "Don't go crazy." I'm afraid that if she gives it up I too will have to commit to giving it up, and I am not ready to do that. "What, Clare? We're already depressed, and now what? We're going to take away the one thing that dependably gives us pleasure? Remember Jonathan Franzen. Don't blame the cards, Clare—use the cards. I myself have a Solitaire practice that is very, very sophisticated. My technique has taken decades to perfect. Only the masters can do it—I call it 'Chasing the Cat.' Simply put, I openly and without shame set up my computer to ping back and forth between my exciting Solitaire game and my boring article. Over the next four hours, it more and more dawns on me that I'm making no work progress, my Solitaire game is getting more frustrating, I now have just forty minutes until my deadline, I'm really screwing up this time. Now comes the strangely pleasurable adrenaline-fueled panic of having procrastinated for too long. . . . And now my day is exciting. And in panic I finish just under the wire. Whee! It's like giving yourself permission to smoke just a little bit of crack!"

"Wow," she says flatly. "Now that's pathetic."

And with the utterance of that telling phrase—"that's pathetic"—oh no, the rosy-hued magic spell of our happiness projects is broken. Because in point of fact, we *are* rather pathetic!

Gym Dandy

CLARE AND I DECIDE to give our happiness projects—
and each other—a break. In the meantime, my menopause
expert, Ann, has informed her friend Isabel of my change-of-
life situation. Isabel says that to fend off her own menopausal
blues, she had tried therapy (expensive), hormones (the bloat),
and even a bevy of natural aids like soy and black cohosh tea
and Saint-John's-wort (ran out of cabinet space in kitchen, had
to expand Whole Foods "library" onto back porch, raccoons—
eventually very mellow raccoons).

"The only thing that worked?" Isabel insists. "Regular
exercise."

I'm not typically a fan of exercise, as I have yet to experience
its reportedly magical endorphin-rushing effects. Then again,
possibly the reason it hasn't worked for me is that my own form
of exercise is doing sudokus—carefully propped up on the
"dashboard," with a mechanical pencil—while walking on a
treadmill so slowly I might as well be sitting.

That said, neither do I feel ready to join Isabel in her clearly mad Groupon offer for "bikini boot camp" that meets in the park every morning at 6:15 A.M.

It's at this point, though, that I am sent on a travel-magazine assignment to visit an eco-spa in Arizona for a weekend "yoga retreat for foodies." It's, at the very least, a tribute to how creative spa marketing directors become in the off-season: The filled-to-capacity workshop is 90 percent women, of whom almost half seem to be celebrating their fiftieth birthdays. It turns out to be light on the yoga and heavy on the small tasting plates. By the third day, indeed, there have been so many witty *amuse-bouches*, edgy dark-chocolate creations, and locally sourced gourmet cocktails like prickly pear margaritas that, what with the Arizona desert water retention, I am finding myself feeling just a bit bloated.

Tucking into yet another arresting appetizer featuring sharp-angled prawns that appear to be on a steeplechase across a field of crostini spattered with goat cheese, I observe humorously to Mr. Y, who has accompanied me, that I am soon going to have to escape the health spa and go home just to be able to fit into my pants.

Mr. Y jovially agrees, drains his glass of wine, goes to the bathroom in the nearby men's lounge, and—apparently just because I have raised the issue—cheerfully leaps onto a scale. To his horrified (and yet still-not-uncheerful WASP) amazement, the number he sees is 195. "I'm stunned," he reports upon returning to the table. He refills his wineglass to calm himself.

"Is 195 a lot?" I ask. I have no idea what Mr. Y should weigh. He looks fine to me, for a man whose idea of exercise is

stooping down over his welcome mat to pick up the Wednesday *New York Times* (the one that contains the Dining section).
I'm at the stage of life where I'm not going to hold anyone—
including myself—to any sort of punishing bar.

"I feel technically that I should weigh 175," he muses. "I
mean in theory, I like to. Back in the day. For me 165 is probably almost too skinny—"

"When were you 165?" I ask, truly surprised.

"Oh, college," he says vaguely. "On the other end of the
dial, 185 feels chubby, definitely chubby. That always feels like
a lot. But 195! Nelly! *Whoa!*"

"Then again," I say, "maybe you dodged a bullet by not
seeing the dreaded two hundred."

"Perhaps so," he agrees as we clink glasses.

Upon thinking it over, I found this whole conversation
extraordinary for two reasons. One was how, as opposed to
women, a man might jump on a scale in the middle of dinner with no preparation at all (dieting, voiding, or making out
a will in case of seeing a truly frightening number). Second was
how, also as opposed to women, men measure their weight in
ten-pound increments. Mr. Y's assessment of his weight was
similar to that performed by most of the men I know: While
they consider a weight of 165 skinny (even for middle-aged
men, the reference point always seems to be college), they don't
generally care either (too much) to bounce around in the low
two hundreds. By my estimation, for a normal-size man, that is
almost a fifty-pound "normal weight" range, and that's without
giving birth to a baby or small heifer in the middle.

The take-home was that Mr. Y was concerned enough to

think that he himself might like to begin exercising, and so, based on another more humane Groupon forwarded by Isabel, we decide to check out Equinox. If you don't know Equinox, let me tell you that these glittering, slightly overpriced, urban yuppie gyms are marvelous. It's a brand that just works. Our local Equinox was located in a luxury condominium complex that also included a microbrewery, a J. Crew, and a Gelson's gourmet supermarket, all one needed for life in one fell swoop, provided you were a microbrew/J. Crew/Gelson's person, which I could well see myself becoming. (Persimmon nail polish— and why not?)

More than a health club, Equinox is a sparkling ship of fun, a kind of Holland America Line cruise ship designed for anxious middle-aged professionals (like moi!) with zero attention span. Upon entry into its eucalyptus-scented interior, we immediately saw a gleaming hive of incredibly fit fifty-something people humming, humming, humming on their tendon machines, as though in some sort of fitness military academy. Almost all looked keenly Lance Armstrong–like (too bad about the steroids) with incredibly lean thighs and papery skin and feathered three-hundred-dollar haircuts. They were in better shape than most twenty-year-olds. Have you seen Kelly Ripa? In contrast to how perfectly petite and sculpted she looks today, twenty years ago she looked like a large blobby muffin.

I have become an expert on Kelly Ripa because of all the midday television playing at Equinox on twenty, thirty monitors at a time, hanging in banks above all the treadmills and the cycles. These flickering eyes into midday America show a nation in a frenzy of activity. Amid the usual windows into the exploding Middle East or the plunging Dow or gaggles of football players mauling one another, you can see ordinary people remodeling homes, hand-making pasta, and competing against one another as they frantically bake cupcakes before a giant red digital timer. One memorable commercial showed a man carrying a flask of his own uric acid in a satchel. I can't tell you why, but he seemed pleased about it. Americans are surfing at fifty, dating at sixty-five, playing rock guitar at eighty. How terrifying! Game on!

The next layer of Equinox fascination was a copy of the weekly exercise-class schedule—a document I started taking to my *As We Change* evening-bath rack to peruse like an intriguing novella. My goodness! Just the language brought to mind a hyperfantastical version of *Logan's Run*, with the difference being that rather than getting killed for the sin of turning thirty, we were all going to get crunched or burned or punked or something. All the instructors had names like Skip and Moon and Keli. The exercise-program names were reminiscent of the CIA or Navy SEALs. I ask you: What is METCON3? TARKL? VIPR?

I think these frightening activities have something to do with intervals, weights, Dynabelts, and the Israeli military, if possibly not in that order. And who were the people, I wondered, who would regularly (ever?) turn up for all these outlandish classes? I mean, sixty minutes of spinning, every weekday morning, at 5:45 A.M.? Good God! I could cycle for an hour, check my stocks, take my cholesterol meds, tweeze my nose hair, and it would still not even be 7:00. My days are already interminably long. To get up before dawn to do something miserable like spinning and then to have even more day left over afterward? Which they wanted to fill with—something? One could only marvel at these people.

More immediately, though, due to confusion about our Equinox "package," Mr. Y and I have somehow ended up buying twelve weeks' worth of individual personal training. (Was it twelve weeks apiece or twelve weeks for two people for a total of six each? I found it difficult to grasp our Equinox finances, as if it was all in a foreign currency.) In any case we decided to embrace the experience, and dutifully appeared on a Wednesday around lunchtime for our first training.

Mr. Y's trainer was an affable Venezuelan named Fabrizio. Mine was a steel-cut Scandinavian named Stef, a twenty-three-year-old with a tiny nose.

The first thing I learned is that today's personal trainers are all into "the core," working "the core." There is also quite a bit of this disturbing thing called "planking." Overall, I have to say that buying personal training seemed a bit like buying an Adelphia cable bundle. You just wanted HBO but it turns out you also have to take Cinemax and Starz. I'd like smaller thighs, but equally urgent to Stef was that we strengthen my woefully weak lats, a part of my body I couldn't even see. So there you go. After twelve weeks of body sculpting I might still have a big if more muscular rear end, but I would also have these amazingly strong invisible underparts of my shoulder blades.

On the upside, instead of sort of vaguely Black Swanning it all day so one can heap all of one's measly fifteen hundred calories into a reasonable dinner, I would now be obliged to eat not just breakfast and lunch every day but carbs. Stef was firm about that. In order to get enough fuel to power through my rigorous new weight-training regimen, I would have to eat carbs. Carbs were back in!

I in fact start needing those carbs because Stef is pushing me so hard—with giddy "games" and "relays" of her own invention, all of which (like so many adult activities) fall just short of "fun"—that I actually start to dread our training sessions. But because of the tireless endurance Equinox trainers have, Stef is merciless about texting constant reminders about our weekly schedule so I can never quite "forget."

Indeed, at one point I actually started thinking, Oh great. To cope with midlife depression, I've signed myself up for a weekly exercise program so demanding that the very idea of it makes me even more depressed. It seemed unfair. I had courageously made the financial commitment (which, when I looked at my Visa bill, gave new meaning to the phrase, "feel the burn"). Now I wanted Stef to go away. Could I gift my twelve training sessions to someone? Sell them on Craigslist? Maybe I could pay Equinox a second fee to get this overeager trainer to now leave me alone.

Then again, thanks to Stef, I was no longer depressed. I was simply scared of my personal trainer, and instead of mortality what I most dreaded in life was our sessions.

I also noticed that while I was grunting with Stef, almost wanting to vomit, just beyond, Mr. Y and Fabrizio could be seen leaning against the pec equipment and discussing local haircutters. Poor Mr. Y. In six weeks (or twelve?) he was still going to have a fluffy soufflé top while I was going to have—as

Stef put it—a "rock-star body." ("*Rock-star body!*" she'd scream, as I hopped through an endless row of tires in a fit of panic.)

Getting more physically confident, 'tis true, I decide it is finally time to check out some of those *Logan's Run* classes. Having a talent for reading between the lines, with a red pen I immediately cross out several obvious problems: Ab Blast, Barre Burn, Tread Shread, Bikini Body Workout, Streamline Sculpt, and Hardbody Meltdown. No sirree. I don't feel that confident. I settle on Yoga Glow, and the more loosey-goosey-sounding Fitness Scramble.

The only problem I find with Fitness Scramble, populated mostly by women and led by a diminutive, fantastically fit blonde in a baseball cap, is that I neglected to have at least three lines of cocaine, or at least some amyl poppers, before starting. In five-minute and thirty-second and sixty-second bursts, over a hip-hop music mix punctuated by the sound of a whip cracking, you rush from station to station working thighs, abs, pecs, glutes, as though on a kind of mad fitness scavenger hunt. I am running about so frantically, bending over, sitting up, lunging back, squatting down, that at one point I feel myself doing what I, a mother of two, can only call a "reverse Kegel."

As for the gear, aside from the standard weights, elastic bands, bars, ropes, and pads, apparently the newest thing in exercise technology is something called the Kettlebell. It's a diabolical little hand weight shaped like a teakettle. Our leader urges us to swing the Kettlebell through the air. I hoist it over my head like a cow tossing its collar. Our teacher further exhorts us to feel the Kettlebell power, to catch Kettlebell fever! Sweating profusely, over the whip cracking and the timer constantly going off, I begin hallucinating. I imagine myself getting a full-blown Kettlebell . . . infection.

Wow! Becoming manic, I am turning into a total exercise-class dilettante. There is no weirdly named exercise class I won't try once. I try Cardio Barre—fifty minutes of "targeted body sculpting" involving little weights you pick up and move in tiny, quarter-size circles, tilting your arm at a precise unpleasant angle, sixty-four times a side. Seven minutes into Cardio Barre I wish for death, but it is an active wish. Much more preferable was Zumba, the Latin (Brazilian?) dance craze! I *cumbia*, I grasp my machete and cut sugarcane, do Bollywood left, Bollywood right, walk like a model, wave my finger back and forth in rhythm to the music and shout, "No more! No more!" When after class I see I have missed another called Cardio Broadway, I let out a Nathan Lane–size falsetto scream!

A Brief Discussion of Manopause

TOP TEN SIGNS YOU ARE GOING
THROUGH MANOPAUSE

Excessive YouTube-ing of old footage of your eighties
  college rock band

Excited remixing of old band tapes—transferring
  cassettes to digital, remixing

Those are really the only two I can think of, as per my
  short attention span.

L ET ME TRY ANOTHER approach in order to address
the men.

CLUB BLAB is in session again. Mr. Y and I are standing
with glasses of wine in the kitchen, gossiping.

I have been asked by Elise—you recall, my angry divorced girlfriend of the ridiculous white-wine bistro—if I can set her up with anyone. I have to admit to her that I know very few eligible—or even ineligible—bachelors. It's sad. All the presentable men I know are married. From experience, that is not a pool I recommend.

"Do you know any single men?" I ask Mr. Y.

We puzzle through the list: Dave? Tom? Albert?

"They're all in manopause," I complain.

"Sam Johnson!" he erupts. "Gainfuly employed, financially solvent, not bad looking—Sam Johnson is totally eligible."

"Sam Johnson?" I retort. "He has been on pause since the age of thirty-seven. And the last time we invited him to something—don't you remember?"

Just the other month I had ten vibrant single forty- and fifty-something women over for dinner. They brought couscous and limoncello and cranberry spread. One woman brought everyone a gorgeous scarf based on their individual color "seasons" out of her new online boutique knitting company. Another demonstrated one-arm planking from circus class, another pole dancing, another some striptease moves (also from class). Someone else confessed her fear of death, a hush fell, then we cried, then we laughed, someone wrote a short blog post about it, she got ten comments, we inked another date in our calendars, all did the dishes, someone shared organic aloe hand lotion samples, someone else got a brainstorm for a new Internet marketing company, and several carpooled home the same way as they had come, to save gas.

It's a little thing we like to call Tuesday.

"You invited Sam," I say to Mr. Y, "but he declined. Remember why?"

"Oh right," he remembers with a start. Sam's exact response, to an invite for dinner with ten vibrant single women: "Why don't you just punch me in the face?"

"But his second reason not to come was that quite honestly the Olympics were on."

"Oh come on, the Olympics?!" I exclaim. "It is streaming over DIRECTV, the Net, my iPhone, and probably the toaster. I saw it in an elevator at Target, and on a Chevron monitor screen while pumping gas. It's actually quite hard to avoid the Olympics. You would have to go to the desert in someplace like Utah to book a room in a windowless U-Haul storage unit. You would have to put on a blindfold and earmuffs. You would have to knock yourself out with twelve Ambien. You would have to make an effort. I wouldn't exactly call it destination viewing."

"Sam very much likes to see things in real time," Mr. Y notes.

"Right, but to put it bluntly: We like Sam a lot, and he has always seemed fairly functional at least in his job, but compared with much of the rest of the human race, Sam is slow."

"Well," Mr. Y admits, "the other reason Sam declined is because he said he 'felt fat.' "

What the—? Manopause!

Parenting Adolescents During Perimenopause, or Medieval Times

A T FORTY-NINE, THE EXPERIENCE of having two pre-teen daughters living in my house is like having a plate-glass window into which two birds are constantly flying—smack! crisis! shrei!—every five minutes. Piercing screams come from the bedrooms over ever-new emergencies. "My *belt*!" "My *zipper*!" "My *chin*!" or "My *shoes*!" That's if they're lucky enough to have two of the same kind of shoe. My daughters and I are all in transitional stages of our development: They preadolescent, I perimenopausal, and so, more often than not, in our volcano-pile household, it's just "My *shoe*!"

Whereas many of our Mad Woman moms had us in their twenties, I, along with many of my Gen X cohorts, birthed my brood in my late thirties and early forties. We sisters in the new menopause are the first generation blessed with the task of guiding our daughters through wild hormonal fluctuations while living through our own. Or as the late great Erma Bombeck used to say: "I'm trying very hard to understand this generation. They have adjusted the timetable for childbearing so that menopause and teaching a sixteen-year-old how to drive a car will occur in the same week." Of course, this is a hopeful notion. It is presuming my daughters get to sixteen.

I remind you that a menopausal woman's hormone levels are the same as a preadolescent girl's. That none of us is fertile means that none of us is consistently firing those magical hormones that we'd like to associate with women, or at least with respectable women. Which is to say we're all thinking of ourselves first, rather than about men or boys we're dating or would like to date, and as such no one is paying much attention to her appearance (or sometimes even hygiene, it seems). Everyone is on her own personal emotional roller coaster, which corresponds not to a moon cycle but to an orbital spray of God knows which planets, some of which inspire us to spend eight hours painting an incomprehensible mural about horses and birthday cake on our own bedroom wall. In addition, without those internal chemicals that promote nurturing, bonding, and nesting, we all lack that magical Doris Day mind-set one needs to cheerfully fold dinner napkins, towels, sheets, and laundry, to cut up vegetables or fruit or bake muffins for other people, or even, particularly, to empty the litter box. Sometimes I feel our house is coming to resemble a boardinghouse for bachelor serial killers.

Granted, I've been living with my girls for a decade already, and it has never been particularly easy. I remember wheeling a double stroller through airports, pumping breast milk in temporary apartments, chasing toddlers across Target parking lots in five different cities. I have endured such sensory violations as lice, peed-on car seats, and five-year-olds' birthday parties at Chuck E. Cheese's. (For those not in the know, Chuck E. Cheese is like Las Vegas for kids, with constant buzzers and bell chimes and coins clattering. For the Chuck E. Cheese mascot think giant mouse, macarena-ing in a baseball cap, whose fur typically appears to be smeared with suet. My daughters were so uncoordinated they would pull their arm back to throw a Skee-ball and it would fly out behind and hit somebody in the back. There is a wine grotto where you literally shove your mug into a wall under a spigot!)

But now that I am forty-nine and perimenopausal, a new horror is dawning on me. Looking back to my early forties, those still-fertile years when my body was suffused with nurturing "love chemicals" like estrogen and oxytocin, I had a thicker protective epidermis—almost like an elephant's hide—against the annoyances that, it turns out, children can be. I had the ability to type coherent text into my computer while around me my children were shout-counting with Dora or Sharpie-mustaching their American Girl dolls or stroking the dog's pelt with my personal hairbrush.

While I love my nine- and eleven-year-old daughters, these days, as I continue to hotflash more and more, there are times when I find it hard to bear the actual sound of their voices. (This reminds me of that very special menopause symptom cited in 1857, called "temporary deafness"—if only!) I pick them up after school and am newly stunned by how quickly my tween daughters speak, how loudly, and at what an incredibly high pitch. There my girls go singing nonsense songs off YouTube, chattering away about who has a crush on whom and, perhaps most irksome of all, eagerly retelling me the plots of their favorite television shows. I believe parents have some obligation to try to listen to our children's thoughts, probably, but I don't believe there's anything in the manual that says we have to listen to them describe the plots of television shows.

Dinner is worse. Back in my previous marriage, when Mr. X was on the road working and it was just me and the girls, I fed them early, sometimes on TV trays. I'd snack later, while making the lunches for the next day. Everything was loose, everything was mellow, and all was well. Unfortunately, in his formal WASP way, Mr. Y believes in a "dinner hour" where everyone sits down at the table at the same time. I think it's a nice idea in theory. But I am a perimenopausal woman with increasing head ringing and hot flashes, and now there are even night sweats. It's like the inside of my head has itself become a Chuck E. Cheese. At forty-nine my strong preference would be to eat dinner at 4:30 in the afternoon in a darkened cave in Antarctica. I have become this kind of hulking, irritated bison who truly wants to be left alone as I eat. To be fair, it's partly because of what I eat. On the rare occasions where Mr. Y lets us do Make Your Own Taco night—he thinks it's boorish to eat with one's hands—out of years of habit I will try to roll up a burrito using lettuce instead of a tortilla. Trembling with hunger because it's already almost 6:00 P.M., when by rights my door should be closed to the world with a Do Not Disturb sign, I jut my jaw forward to bite into the collapsing thing. Tomatoes are dropping, it's a losing battle—and when my teeth close against each other, half the construction falls onto my neck—and now my entire household starts pointing at me and laughing ("Mommm! How gross!").

"Good God!" I exclaim, standing and picking up my plate. "I love all of you very dearly, but I can't stand another minute with you!"

BUT IF you're the perimenopausal mother of a tween, the trouble runs deeper than all that.

It's tough in middle age in general to be an old dog learning new electronic tricks. My thumbs are too fat to write texts on my iPhone, and my eyes are too dim to read them. I don't know how to turn off the Kindle, so when planes are taking off I frantically take a pillow and "smother" it. There is no device upon which my girls won't keep playing with the ring tones, so when the next thing goes off I find myself feeling completely addled—was that my phone, is there a space-alien invasion, or has the microwave finished some popcorn? And do the space aliens want some?

But in fact none of this has prepared me for the peculiar horrors of Facebook. When Hannah first introduced it into our lives I was neither aware of what to do with Facebook, nor of the fact that one is not even supposed to be on Facebook until the age of thirteen (Hannah is eleven). Never mind. My own Facebook account seemed to exist only for the purpose of enabling me to peer into the relatively benign world of my keyboard-tapping daughter and her out-of-town cousins. As I've experienced it, preteen Facebook is typically a sleepy, as-innocuous-as-a-Christmas-letter world of angsting about the English paper due tomorrow while qvelling about the latest funny cat photo, finished off with a curt BRB or GTG (Be

Right Back or Got To Go). My daughter's set are the sorts of kids who friend their grandparents and aunts and uncles, the better to accost them to buy candy bars for the school PE program fund-raiser. Even Internet predators would have to struggle to stay awake through the continual pelting of trivia, as relentless as an avalanche of stuffed animals.

One night, while I'm writing at the computer . . . well, to this day I cannot account for how this happened. Perhaps it was a temporary glitch or experiment Facebook was trying. I swear to God, all I know is I was sitting there at my computer, and suddenly on the right side of my screen I saw this conversation unrolling in real time. It appeared to stem from a post on a page of one of my daughter's friends (he posted a photo of what appeared to be a badger in a Dodgers cap). Perhaps I was seeing this post because my daughter opened her Facebook account on my computer, and hence when she opened one for me there was a period of strange hybridization between our two identities. Even today my Facebook page states that I am a fan of Bruno Mars, Starbucks Mochachinos, and Keyboard Cat, all artifacts of my daughter's. So I can't account for the mysterious mechanics of this, but suddenly, scrolling down the right half of the screen, in real time, is a Lord of the Flies comment thread of sixth-graders "flaming" my completely wide-eyed and innocent Hannah, she of the leotards, goofy glasses, and angel wings.

The thread is something like:

J33T: Here's my funny cat photo.

JAZZ12: LOL!

KK: GTG!

11YEAROLD "DJ" RONALD K: Ha ha ha.

[SUDDEN AD FOR "FARMVILLE"—WHATEVER THAT IS]

J33T: JK, jk.

[SANDRA'S OVERLY IMAGINATIVE AND VULNERABLE 11-YEAR-OLD DAUGHTER HANNAH]: LOL You've been BOBBED! [Another joke emoticon of some kind]

GEORGE12: OMG, Hannah—being Bobbed is so OVER!

[SOIAVEYODH]: OMG, George . . . Why are you being so MEAN????

LILI: Oh Hannah don't be such a spaz.

J33T: How about my funny cat photo

KK: jk.

JAZZ12: LOL.

[SUDDEN AD FOR STARBUCKS HAZELNUT BLIZZARDS—APPEARS TO BE A TWO-FOR-ONE COUPON]

GEORGE12: Why are you so WEIRD, Hannah?

LILI: ROTFL [Actually this is wrong—ROTFL is only one of the ones I remember—she probably put something down like @#$@1234ff3. Whatever it was, it was clearly dismissive and meant to hurt.]

[SOIAVEYODH]: I am not weird you guys! I've changed since fifth grade! I have LOTS of friends now! [My poor sweet baby! She is in sixth grade now at a new school, a more sensitive performing-arts academy that better suits her fragile personality.]

GEORGE12: LOL.

JAZZ12: Why did you use to chew your hair in science, Hannah? That was weird.

LILI: Agree with g.

[SOIAVEYODH]: LOOK IN THE MIRROR It's you guys who are WEIRD!!!!!

GEORGE12: LOL. Said by someone who's FACEBOOK FRIENDS WITH HER MOMMY!!!!

I go upstairs. I physically pull my daughter off her laptop—aka out of the burning building. We sit on her bed, she weeps with the hurt of it, I form a body block around her, easily (the large fleshly cape of me), and I shore her up. This is easy to do in the moment.

In the twenty-first century there is no lack of parental discussion of bullying. There is a national antibullying movement. There is probably a Facebook page against bullying, possibly an app, and in all likelihood a Pepsi-Cola Kickstarter page sponsored by Ryan Seacrest. Furthermore, for us former-nerds-turned-creative-class-parents, there is no lack of sage aphorisms about bullying with which you can enlighten your children. One can begin with the easy softball—mocking the mean kids' (inevitably laughable) spelling (instead of TTYL—Talk To You Later—they may get the letters mixed up: TYTL). You can say, roundly, and with pretty provable meritocratic confidence, "Such a rocket scientist as George12 will surely be serving me slaw in eight years at the Sherman Oaks El Pollo Loco!" You can also say: "You know who was bullied? Lady Gaga! Her high-school peers shoved her into a trash can, she invented a fabulous dress out of trash, and now she is an international rock star worth twenty-two billion!" And amazingly enough, it is true!

In short, drying her tears, my daughter is able to dust herself off, have dinner, finish her homework, read a book, work on one of her fairy-tale dragon stories, pop onto Facebook one last time to post a funny cat photo, and go to bed, snoring soundly. In the morning, in one of her spectacularly odd middle-school costumes (hoodie, bathrobe, hair in pigtails tied with orange pipe cleaners), she will cheerfully sail out again, like the ever-optimistic Fool of card 0.

While of course, her perimenopausal forty-nine-year-old mother lies awake until 4:16 A.M., wide-eyed with worry.

I stare at the ceiling, my gaze penetrating into darkness as my hot flashes rage with surging and dropping hormones. I know from modern parenting books that my generation is sternly advised not to become hovering, overprotective helicopter parents. And certainly middle school has long been awful. Middle school is the pack of wolves surrounding the hapless lamb crumpling in slow-motion tears under his or her backpack. It was, in my own case, the proud handstand performed at the eighth-grade talent show, the too-tight white pants suddenly ripping, the wobbling, veering side-crash, ending in a grotesque fart. It was the bouquet of dead flowers shoved into one's mailbox, with parodic "Hallmark card" courtesy—hey, thanks!—of the popular kids.

Suddenly I am recalling the time I myself ran for seventh-grade treasurer—a post literally no one else wanted but that as a geek I was thrilled to campaign for. My campaign featured hand-drawn posters, the design cribbed from a corporate health campaign at Hughes Research, where my father worked. I lovingly traced the image with a gizmo called a pantograph. I remember how in Mr. Vincent's fifth-period government, Jodi Schneekling (can't you just tell by the name? Schneekling?)—

she of the Farrah Fawcett flip, Kork-Ease sandals, Chemin de Fer jeans with laces crossed in front, like the secret Masonic sign of some evil tween dungeon mistress—turned toward me. "Let's see that poster," Jodi said. Flattered at her interest (she was popular!), I flopped it open to her. It was drawn in ten different colored pens, with the catchy tagline: "It's harder to get a rhino to rumba than to have a great year without electing Sandra Loh for 7th grade class treasurer!"

Jodi looked at it, slitted her eyes, leaned toward me across our desks, and whispered: "Sandra? I wouldn't vote for you if you were the last person on earth."

Peculiar historical note: Elected boys' vice president of our whole school that year was a popular surfer named Sean Penn—oh yes, the very same. Sean Penn was widely regarded as affable and easygoing. That's right. Compared with me, Sean Penn? Affable.

So all right, yes, these are the sorts of things a normal person would laugh off three decades later. But what I experience instead, as I hotflash in the night, is the explosion of my emotions for my daughter and for my eleven-year-old self into a single, palpable, slowly burning-upward spine flame. The future and the past are one and the same as I burn with rage and hormones. Fertility's heightened levels of estrogen supposedly calm the parts of the brain that experience hurt and agitation when slights are perceived. Supposedly that's because it is not evolutionarily useful for mothers to harbor grudges over past injustices when they should be expending energy nurturing others and preparing them for the future. But, of course, neither my daughter nor I are processing those chemicals. Our insults (past and present) are raw, and without that protective estrogen coating—fasten your seat belts!

"Stop chewing your fingernails," Mr. Y murmurs, slapping my hand away from my mouth as I lie awake at 3:23 A.M. "Just because your eleven-year-old has one bad experience, you don't have to negatively anticipate what's going to happen to her over the next seven years."

"True enough—of course not," I say. "That would be ridiculous, overcatastrophizing." (Note canny use of multisyllabic therapy word.) "Except, except, except . . ." I stare into the blackness.

"Why is there never a consequence?" I push on. "Oh no, in the decades beyond, the George12s of the future will reappear at some twentieth high-school reunion as a bland realtor or similar, having no memory of the incident, only dispensing matchbooks with the name of their realty company that everyone is connected to via linkedin.com! As we all turn increasingly gray."

I hear a snore.

Why I train like an Olympian with Stef and subsequently can't sleep, while Mr. Y laconically trades hair tips with Fabrizio and sleeps as if he has just done the Pyrenees leg of the Tour de France, I don't know.

With Mr. Y unconscious, I continue to worry. Alone in the night, I can't help but wonder: Am I passing down some legacy that should have stopped with me to my child? Am I infecting my child with my own uncoolness? Look at George's statement: "Said by someone who's FACEBOOK FRIENDS WITH HER MOMMY!!!!" My daughter is clearly too damn open, and trusting, and unashamedly close to me—she has no protective middle-school shell.

In being too good a friend to my daughter, have I helped her self-esteem rise a bit too nosebleedingly high? Look at those exotically ragtag outfits she invents, and runs around in! My daughter has no lack of loving, nurturing adults in her life, who enable her to go to museums and the theater and Cirque du Soleil and encourage to her write fantasy stories. Not only do I approve of said fantasy stories, I also help her arrange them in antique fonts. What kind of training is this for the real world? This smothering attachment parenting is evidently piss-poor preparation for sixth grade and for the George12s of the world. But then I realize something else.

"Facebook friends with your mommy"?

George12, you have made a fatal mistake. Cue Darth Vader music.

Because if Mommy is on Facebook, she can read in real time what everyone is typing—including you, George12. And while the word "mommy" suggest a nice lady in a housedress with a tray of nummy-nummy muffins, this mommy is deep into perimenopause, and she doesn't have any estrogen left (the hormone that makes mommies "nice"). My womb is so empty one need only brush aside the cobwebs to make room for *the tool kit of medieval hurt I'm going to bring down.*

Let's just say I have known George12 ever since he wept and peed in his pants his first day in kindergarten. This mommy's fanny pack contains iPhone photos of George12 at the Cheese-cake Factory from back when all the kids were still real friends, when I bought George12 not just a deluxe pizza and red-velvet cheesecake but, if memory recalls, a *second* Cherry Coke. This mommy knows quite a few of George12's secrets, like— something that would surprise his famously conservative, Arme-nian, limo-driving dad—his penchant for musical theater.

I am actually hyperventilating with anger. It is as if I've taken five hits of testosterone and nine of crack. I've never done crack, but I assume this is what it feels like. Need I remind you that during the change, testosterone does not wane? In some women it actually rises.

Which is not to say that this mommy's anger-management issues are new. Oh no: These were in full swing even when Han-nah was in her crunchy-granola preschool, where a philosophy of "nonviolent conflict resolution" backfired and spawned a literal axis of four-year-old evil. One day the play yard bully—Andy Johnson—pulled this "Mommy" down and started punch-ing her in the face. When the other crunchy-granola parents weren't looking (they were hand-grinding organic hummus) I picked the kid up, pinned his arms back, and whispered, very, very quietly: "Andy? You punch me again and I'll kick you in the stomach *so hard you'll wish you'd never lived*."

In short the question is not Am I going down to the school-yard to take this twelve-year-old out, it's Which ball gown shall I wear?

Content with my savvy plan of action, sometime before 5:00 A.M. I fall asleep.

. . .

AT 2:52 P.M. the next day I am sitting on a bench in front of George12's sixth-period classroom. I am wearing jeans, boots, and aviator glasses, and I have put on goth-dark lipstick. For a divorced forty-nine-year-old mother, our impending confrontation qualifies as a "date." I have caved before so many bullies before in my life that it is urgent that today I call this asshole out. Hannah's honor—and mine—depends on it.

As I wait, I get a text from Clare: "Sandra? If your preteen basically seems okay and you are the one lying awake at 3:16 angsting, is it about the kid or is it about you? Do you think you are perhaps—oh, what's the phrase?—perimenopausally overreacting?"

I close the text box.

I watch three middle-school boys lounging in front of the bathroom. They sport shaved heads, bad skin, and patchy facial hair. What an ungainly age! The youths are talking and laughing and punching each other, like the overhopped young bucks they are. Outside of Facebook, I think, George12 certainly has his own middle-school work laid out for him, down this echoing Escher-like row of lockers. Cue Sondheim, "Send in the Clowns."

I explain that I am sitting outside George's classroom, waiting for him to come out of sixth-grade English so I can throw him down on the ground and punch him in the face, hard.

Hannah flies into a panic: "Please, please, *please*, Mom, don't do that! I will be *so* embarrassed!"

"He won't get away with this," I declare coldly.

Her tone goes not colder but hotter, tipping into a kind of intense tween hysteria.

"Mom, if you do anything like that? I *swear* I am going to unfriend you!"

Heh?

So I put my gun down.

I simply rat George out to the assistant principal—and how fortuitous the timing! It's Bullying Awareness Month in the LAUSD—and call it a day.

MY SISTER, Kaitlin, visits and dispenses her usual wisdom. In Pema Chödrön mode, she is just giving great, great sister. The nuggets of comfort and wisdom conversation she's giving are just so, so good. It's like buttah. Or artisanally hand-carving a melon in an ingenious way you never thought possible. Look at how brilliantly Kaitlin turns this.

Of Hannah's suffering at the hands of bullying middle-schoolers, Kaitlin says:

1. "What a wonderful opportunity to begin to help your daughter acquire the tools she will need all her life."
2. "Congratulations—how developmentally appropriate—middle school is where the crucial character building for adulthood starts to happen."

And finally—perhaps a bit over the top, but it still lands nicely and salves my wounds:

3. "Children pick their parents—there is a reason you are her mother. I am so pleased my niece has such involved and loving care."

Soothed by her warmth and kindness, I continue to warble: "Middle school is pretty rough for me right now, given my lack of emotional insulation. The other day Hannah was weeping, her face turned to the wall. It was because her former besties, Chloe and Michelle, have moved their seats in English class. The three of them used to sit together, but now Chloe and Michelle have moved to the back. And then to the left. And then to the back again. For twenty minutes Hannah drew it for me, the elaborate ever-changing seating chart. I could feel the pain of each move all too well. It was like the shifting and squeezing of my own internal organs. It's not that I care too little, it's that I care too much! I have such outsize emotional reactions these days, I don't know how I'm going to make it to seventh grade!"

"Oh there, there," she says.

"Sometimes I think dads are better than moms at dealing with this. A dad friend told me recently how his seventh-grade son was approached by a kid after school who handed him a folded-up note. It said: 'The entire 7th grade class has voted and 90% of the class thinks you are weird.' To which his unfazed dad jokingly said, 'What? Just 90 percent thought you were weird? You didn't get 100? Work harder!' His son laughed!"

"Oh, funny," Kaitlin says.

I ask her in bewilderment, "Did we ever tell Mama when we were bullied?"

"Oh God no!" she exclaims. "I mean"—she thinks about it—"it's just . . . You never told your mother things like that. You never wanted to burden her."

"That's right," I agree. "I was bullied all the time at Malibu Park Junior High."

"Oh sure," she agrees matter-of-factly. "I remember these two guys who told me for three straight years, every day on the bus, that because my skin was brown I looked dirty."

"Sure," I say. "But telling Mama—that would be like confessing to something really shameful. I was afraid I would depress her further by admitting that I wasn't really popular at school. I tried to assure her that I was popular, but of course I wasn't. By contrast Hannah tells me everything about middle school, even stuff I don't want to know. I take too much to heart stuff she doesn't even remember the next day."

My sister nods thoughtfully.

"I think Hannah is basically okay and that you can relax a little around this transitional time. You know? Let her have those experimental conversations!"

"Those what?" I ask.

"Whoops," Kaitlin says, furrowing her brow. "Maybe this is one of those secrets she said absolutely not to tell you?" She shakes her head. "*Meh*—I can't keep track. Anyway, apparently Hannah says at school she is experimenting with different ways of having a conversation. Like sometimes, when her friends are talking about boys, which Hannah is not interested in, she will suddenly interrupt and say loudly, 'I'm really bored with this!' and will flounce away. Hannah says she is also experimenting with this really loud British-accented voice, based on the nanny of those kids in that show."

"What show?"

"I don't know—I try to block a lot of this out."

"She sounds sometimes maybe a little histrionic," I admit.

"I wonder where she gets that?" says Kaitlin.

I AM depositing some laundry on that horn of laundry plenty known as Hannah's bed. I notice that hidden behind her headboard she has penciled the word "SADNESS," augmented by a row of about a dozen tears. That's the final straw. I snap.

I go and get her immediately. She is cheerfully cutting out Internet cat photos and using a lot of Scotch tape from the dispenser that is supposed to live on my "desk" (the dining room table). On top of her open science book is a striped legging and the wrapper from an ice-cream sandwich.

"Hannah," I inform her in no uncertain terms. "I know you are a preteen and you are going through a tough transitional time, emotionally."

"Uh-huh," she says guardedly.

"It's like this," I say in exasperation. "*So am I*. Listen, everybody has a different kind of mother! I've done a lot of reading about this. There is the difficult mother, the reactive mother, and the envious mother. I of course had a depressed mother. And right now you have a mother who is going through that thing right now, perimenopause, which means you have a medieval-times mother. Everything for me right now is medieval times. George12 brings dishonor upon you, I ride my horse to George12's castle and disembowel him with a giant spiked metal ball on a chain, singing lusty Gaelic chantey tunes the whole time and I twirl his spraying intestines above my head. Like with my middle-aged Volvo, I don't have a temperature or emotional thermostat that actually works.

"This means that if you are going to noodle around and do teen-goth things like penciling 'SADNESS' on your wall with a row of arty tears, you'd better be prepared to be yanked out immediately of that ridiculous performing-arts middle school you are in where half the class is named Savannah or Chloe and to be transferred immediately instead to Van Nuys Middle School where everyone is either a six-foot-tall Latino or Armenian or Egyptian boy with tats and where I will put you in seventh-grade Running. You'll be on the running team! Either that or I am going to lock you up until you turn forty, and I am not joking around. I mean it. *Capisce?*"

"I love my school!" she cries out in alarm. "No! And I'm actually not that sad! I was just experimenting with drawing eyes!"

"Well, missy," I say. "Then you'd better pull it together. You are simply going to have to manage your emotions like a school extra-credit project. If you want a teen-goth wall, fine, put it up, but really go big with it. Don't do something sad like pencil it on a hidden place on your wall because that alarms me. And also please take down that ridiculous mood meter on your Facebook page because there is only room for exactly one moody person here, and that is your mother. Who is the biggest middle-schooler of all? Your mother! So toughen up, TTYL and BRB!"

So in the end we two infertile and possibly "unfeminine" females shake hands, step over our piles of laundry, and go downstairs to make popcorn, which we douse with Tabasco and chili powder while discussing the fascinating architecture of the dishes piled in the sink, which neither of us chooses to wash at that moment. We may not have solved all of middle school's problems, but there's a temporary truce over the battle-field, and in an hour there will be a new episode of *Family Guy*. We will continue to take an elaborate break from the chores of discussing our feelings. Which in a way is a kind of female liberation.

Bench Warrant for My Father's Arrest

THANK GOODNESS, GIVEN THE wreck I've made of my midlife, I have someone solid to depend on, regarding the futures of my daughters. Thank God there is Grandpa, standing by with his wisdom, support, concern, and, last but not least—money.

Oh but wait a minute—no!

Which is to say, a call now comes from Grandpa. It is not, as one might hope, an announcement that he is transferring new funds into his granddaughters' college accounts. Rather, he asks, could I rush out to Malibu to help him? There appears to be a bench warrant for his arrest.

LET US pause for a moment of explanation.

My eighty-eight-year-old, thrice-divorced, retired Chinese engineer father is the local Malibu eccentric. He has the unkillable disposition and leathery constitution of a lizard. (His resting pulse rate is something like 34.) His cheapness is legendary: It goes beyond frugality into actual sport. He doesn't just hitchhike, he Dumpster-dives (it may be expired grocery sushi, but it's free!). When my mom was still around, when she was running in her lipstick and heels and my dad was disappearing daily into his aerospace job, our family had to hold it together—sort of. Sure there were beakers of green tea bubbling like in a mad scientist's lab on the stove and stacks of his company washroom's stolen paper towels in our bathrooms. Sure my parents fought (always about money), but my mother maintained at least a physical order. The fridge was full, the beds were made, and overall our 1964 Southern California tract house was gleaming. However, now my mother is gone, my elderly dad still lives at home, and sad to say, the house has never been updated or even really cleaned. In a sort of Miss Havisham–style, the family house still has the same sparkling cottage-cheese ceilings, 1964 sunburst linoleum, grease-spattered—and that's several decades of grease—O'Keefe and Merritt stove, and cracked glass shower stalls, since repaired with duct tape. It's the sort of a home where you might find a broken toilet currently being used as a planter. I say "might" as I have not dared to enter a bathroom there since the (first) George Bush administration.

Who lives in the house? For a while it was my dad alone. But then he started to get lonely. Having as we did wildly mixed feelings about growing up there, given how constantly my parents argued and how unhappy our mother grew, it's not as if Kaitlin and I made it a point to visit often. So when my father reached his seventies, he decided he should procure a new Chinese immigrant wife to help him into his dotage.

As opposed to "difficult" Western women, like my German mother had turned out to be, an obedient Chinese wife would accept the distinctly nonfeminist role of cutting up his fruit and massaging his bunions in exchange for U.S. citizenship. And indeed, after several spectacular misfires, on his third try he found Alice. A Manchurian twenty years younger than himself, Alice was able to bear him, it seemed, because of a particular innocence and sweetness of her own that allowed her simply to block him out when he started raging (often).

In addition to Dumpster-diving, a love for which they shared, the thrifty Chinese couple soon cobbled together yet a new cash-positive scheme: renting out Kaitlin's and my bedrooms and even the den in their Miss Havisham house to boarders. Where did they list the ad? Craigslist, of course. Do I help him post listings? Yes—because it's something I can do from a distance, and the longer he thrives in his murky ecosystem the longer I can stay away. Is there a vetting process besides seeing if a check will clear? No. So we've had some problems. Once, when I posted a listing with the clearly too-optimistic title "For the Adventurous Beachcomber!" to my surprise I got a deluge of letters from people frantic to spend $550 a month to live in my dad's (eerily not pictured—which I thought was a dead giveaway) hellhole. These eager renters were, almost to the last man, twenty-nine-year-old British construction engineers from London—by unusual coincidence, too, all were nonsmoking Scorpio vegetarians who had to get out of the UK immediately due to the strict requirements of their twelve-month construction contract and who thus all wanted to rush me cashier's checks for two months' advance rent. In short, they were Nigerians.

Even more exotic, however, were the renters who were not scams. There was the transsexual alcoholic whose operation was apparently not 100 percent totally completely successful. He/she would call me at home late at night and accuse me of trying to steal his/her identity. There have been sixty-something beachcombers, vitamin sellers, hollow-eyed Manson-looking types on disability. There have been knife fights at midnight over misplaced sprouters and juicers (vegans can be very edgy). There has been some lightly botched drug dealing. One guy was a diabetic (he said) who left an explosion of blood and medical supplies in the kitchen.

Kaitlin has described my father's place as less halfway house than all-the-way house.

Then again, some of the tenants are "pretty nice." Overall, barring some of the obvious spectacular misfires, my dad says he generally enjoys his tenants' company.

And what do I say? I say fantastic. It may not be pretty, but if you saw their spreadsheets, you would know that my dad and Alice are actually making money. They're completely independent. They are continuing to sock away cash. Dumpster-dive away!

But of course now the first wrinkle in this madcap Craigslist adventure is apparently this bench warrant. The bench warrant, I learn, is because Janice, a former renter, apparently had a yappy dog even though my dad claims vociferously she was not supposed to. There is little way of confirming anyone's side of this story. My father is my father, and Janice was, I recall, the sort of tenant given to writing notes to other tenants literally on paper towels. Here is a sample excerpt (because I track all the paperwork) to a fellow tenant named Douglas:

> You don't need to know that God made my receptors-magnetic field down When I get BAD HEADACHES the medicine changes me May God strike you down with the DEVILS BIBBLE after the other day you told me all about your GIRLFRIEND MARIA and I heard you with her Doing It with ur marijuana muffins and CRYSTAL PILLS??? Dr. Loh's house is all your dishes dishes dishes cups and cigarettes GET A LIFE Is rooted in you Americans—Me—Me—Me. Lost my dog Pebbles and then lee came behind me call me a WHORE f— YOU!!!

Bottom line, Janice got into some sort of altercation with my father, she accused him of harassing her dog, and then she threw a lawsuit against him with a court summons. Thanks to the advice of his legal counsel (a mellower tenant with a few years of law school who was a practitioner of the Bahai religion), my father did not bother showing up. But unfortunately this was like traffic court: No matter how whimsical the charges, you have to show up, otherwise you owe the suer fourteen hundred dollars, which my father now owes Janice. He hasn't paid it, and that's why there is a bench warrant for his arrest.

. . .

I ARRIVE at 10:00 A.M. on a Monday at the Malibu courthouse, over an hour's drive from my home. My father looks pretty close to a bag person today. His unmatched clothes hang limply, he carries his usual "briefcase" of a brown paper shopping bag, his unshaved gray beard looks, no way around it (shaving accident?), a tad bloody. He shuffles a bit with his Parkinson's—sometimes he uses a wheelchair, though not today. Alice sits next to him, anxious, birdlike, fuzzy black Smurf-doll hair, in strange girl-doll clothes with white socks in tiny buckled sandals. She carries a clearly repurposed Abercrombie & Fitch bag.

On the other side of the courtroom, several rows behind, is Janice. Her shoulder-length hair is wet and severely combed back; her eyes are red, her mouth is grim, and she is dressed in a wrinkled gray business suit.

Judge Connor calls the court to order, and summons my father and his ex-tenant to their respective stands. My father wrongly believes that this is his cue to heatedly argue his case. Bench warrants aside, he enjoys a good lawsuit. To be sued is to know you're alive. (At one point both of his previous Chinese wives had thrown million-dollar liens against his house, but as a precautionary measure, he had already gotten his kids to throw million-dollar liens against him first, so the ex-wives won't get anything. I think.) My father immediately begins bellowing a mile a minute about how terrible this woman Janice is, what a bad tenant, what a criminal, and how menacing her dog Pebbles.

Judge Connor stops him cold.

"That's all well and good, Mr. Loh. But that has nothing

to do with the fact that a court date was set and you failed to appear. There is nothing I can do about it. By county law the fine is fourteen hundred dollars. It is not my decision to make. It's county law. How are you going to pay this fine, Mr. Loh?"

The ensuing dialogue has a predictable rhythm—the sort of circular cadences one associates with small children.

My dad: "But blah, blah, blah! Over and over again I told her about that dog! Bad tenant! Bad tenant! Blah, blah, blah! You should have heard the barking—"

Judge Connor: "Yes I know, Mr. Loh. But the case is closed. Sir, how are you going to pay this fine?"

My dad: "Oh but blah, blah, blah! Late with her checks! Oil-leaking car! Terrible disco music!"

Judge Connor: "Mr. Loh. As I said, it doesn't matter. How are you going to pay this fine?"

My dad: "But Mr. Judge! I am an old man! I need quiet! I need ice cream! Where is the ice cream?" My corns! My bunions! The nation of Islam! Seventeenth-century Flemish haberdashery!" (You see the general point I am making—he is getting more and more worked up about matters entirely unrelated to today's case.)

Judge Connor: "As I said, the fine is fourteen hundred dollars. How do you plan to pay that today?" Repeat loop eleven times. Eventually my father runs out of gas. Perhaps he has not consumed enough calories from the Dumpster to draw this all out into a second hour. When the judge finally threatens to cut him off, he delivers his final braying statement:

"I won't pay it because I can't. I am poor! I am an old man, I have no car, and I eat out of the garbage." I do a quick calculation of just how severely he has perjured himself. The last three statements are, yes, technically true. However, he does own a paid-off house in Malibu, although arguably it is a teardown. That said, due to his penny-pinching habits, he has accumulated all that cash. Were I to point this out he could—and would—respond: "Well, but where is it? Eugene Loh has no money!" And that, of course, is also true.

This is because he has transferred a great deal of his money into accounts bearing my name—I don't know exactly how much, as he has forged my signature for so many years now to evade the tax consequences. I only tend to discover that my name is first on things via the occasional odd penalty notice from the IRS.

Judge Connor terminates the proceedings and dispatches a nonsmiling African American lady bailiff to give my dad some forms. My father hands the forms to me with a trembling hand. I look at them. They are requesting disclosure of all of his bank information—names, branches, accounts, routing numbers—as well as such personal data as his social security number. He is to write down all this information and give it to red-eyed Janice so she can go after his assets personally (CRYSTAL PILLS! BAD HEADACHES! THE DEVILS BIBBLE!).

Mechanically, because the judge has requested it, I begin to fill out the forms for my dad. But then I stop and think: What am I doing? Pen in hand, I am getting that feeling in my chest—the involuntary aorta squeeze, the fluttery palpitations, the shortness of breath. It might be the change of life, or it might be an actual *reasonable cortisol-firing stress response*. I realize that if we fill out this form we can well lose everything, every cent of it, including the house (even just the Malibu land must be worth—what?—half a million?), over a silly fourteen-hundred-dollar fee.

I realize how much I have been counting on my dad's money being there, how much I have expected some kind of inheritance one day and college tuition help for my kids. It is a vague kind of—I don't know—remote distant financial island I have been swimming toward all my life. It has lent a sense of emotional security, a sense of not being left abandoned.

And now? Over a single crazy tenant?

I step into the hallway to call Kaitlin.

"What should I do here?" I ask. "Instead of having him disclose his social security number and all of his personal bank account information to an insanely litigious person, isn't it simpler if I just write the fourteen-hundred-dollar check myself and give it to the judge? Without telling Papa, of course." We know that with our father it's not about not having the money, it's a matter of principle. Pretty much giving anyone any money at all for any reason offends his sense of justice. And this is bad tenant Janice! Rather than give up a dime, he would prefer to come to court every day for a year. As I said, he loves a lawsuit, even if he loses.

My sister is having yet another of her amazing Pema Chödrön days. She is able to look deeply into the prism of her own long experience with our dad to give some extraordinarily wise advice. "Walk away," she intones. "Walk away. He's a lizard. He has his own ways. Getting involved just pulls you into the muck and won't solve anything. You have to just let it go, let it happen."

Some stories have an elegant shape to them. Sadly this is not one of them. Which is to say what happens is that I give the forms back to my dad, crying out with an awkward angry bleat, "I can't help you!" My father takes the forms and stubbornly begins to fill them out with his shaky spotted hand, and I leave. Somehow the whole procedure sort of trails off, and another court date is set.

WHICH IS to say—yes, people—three months later on another Monday morning at ten we are all back at the Malibu courthouse again. The principals arrive, three months older and in different and wilder outfits (Janice has dropped the business wear and is in what I can only describe as a paisley gypsy skirt and space-age turban; Alice appears to be oddly in one brown and one black shoe), and the exact same proceedings occur. Again my father steps up to the podium with his exact same braying speech, again the judge (same judge) reminds him that he is here for one reason and for one reason only—to pay Janice fourteen hundred dollars.

Do you see what I am saying?

As if in a dream, we are here again.

I have sometimes come to feel, in midlife, as though my life is in a loop. I have stared out of my car window at an El Pollo Loco parking lot, waiting for my dad to finish going to the bathroom or something, and have literally seen paint dry. Literally! Seen. Paint. Dry! While my body ripples up and down in flame.

Anyway, again my father and the judge have their interchange. Again the humorless black lady bailiff brings forward exactly the same form. Again my father and Alice murmur, and peck at their brown paper and Abercrombie & Fitch bags in bewilderment. The shaky pen drops. The effort grinds to a halt. Once again.

Now the judge calls Alice forward. "Mrs. Loh?" he asks. "Do you have a checking account?"

"Ye-e-es," she says, in her unsure English.

"Where?" he asks.

"Bank of America?" she replies.

"*The Bank of America on Point Dume?*" Judge Connor asks, as though speaking to a hearing-impaired person.

"Point Dume," she says. "Yes?"

"And, Mrs. Loh, do you have a savings account?"

"Chase," she says. "Malibu. Chase."

And now, without changing his expression, Judge Connor turns to Janice and says: "Ms. Kolakowski, I am satisfied that you have enough information you need to go secure your payment."

Janice's face turns white.

"What? What about his social security number?"

"No, Ms. Kolakowski," Judge Connor replies, friendly yet firm. "I am satisfied that you have all the information you need to approach the Lohs directly for the money they owe you. Best of luck." He raps his gavel.

My father stands still for a moment, ingesting this sudden turn. Then he erupts.

"Oh *thank you!*" my father bellows operatically. While a slow mover, he is a very quick thinker. "Oh *thank you*, oh wise and intelligent judge! You're a very intelligent and honorable man, not like that *bad tenant* Janice—"

"That's enough, Mr. Loh," the judge says curtly, rapping his gavel again, harder.

And that is the end of the bench warrant.

What—?

One take-home is that, if you're going to violate the law, do it in Malibu.

The second is that, upon reflection, I have to acknowledge some grudging admiration for my father's Byzantine techniques. It is not just my signature my father has forged to open checking accounts but those of elderly mothers-in-law in remote parts of China who are actually dead. This is the brilliance of ghost checking accounts. If dead Chinese people—with unpronounceable names like Xi and Qi—are on a checking account that only my father knows exists, and that only he has the paper checks to . . . Well, I'm telling you—as opposed to how everything online today is in danger of being hacked, it's actually an amazingly secure system.

The third take-home is probably the best, though. It's a story my sister shared when I gave her the final report.

"Ah!" she says. "It reminds me of the Chinese folktale I once heard. A restaurant owner was upset by the fact that above his restaurant lived a poor student. Every night the poor student would eat his simple bowl of rice but would be able to smell the aromas of the delicious food being cooked below him. The restaurant owner believed the student should pay him a fee for the privilege. The judge heard the case, and then asked the student to come forward. 'Do you have any money on you?' Whimpering, the student said he had very little, emptying his pants of just a few copper coins. The judge took the coins and passed them back and forth between his hands three times. Then he handed the coins back to the student. 'So there,' he said, to the restaurateur. 'For the smell of food, you've just enjoyed the sound of money!' "

And this is why I enjoy the taste of vodka.

Which is to say his money is safe for another day.

But little do we know how those days are numbered.

Losing It

WHILE MANY AMERICAN WOMEN are obsessed with their weight, I, for one, am calmly and happily not, thank God. Can you imagine? On top of everything else?

This is because after spending forty-nine years together, my weight and I have finally struck a deal. Yes, by necessity, we still cohabitate. We eat together, we sleep together, I still drive the two of us—somewhat heavily—around town. But it doesn't ask after me, and I don't ask after it. You've seen my life. I have enough on my plate without having to worry about that next volatile personality, my weight.

In the eighties and even the nineties, we used to check in anxiously with each other every day, in a minute-by-minute dialogue. But over the decades, with our far-too-close relationship, my weight and I have become increasingly dissatisfied with each other.

My weight is clearly disappointed with my inability to ingest only eight glasses of water and some steamed broccoli a day, and makes its displeasure known by eternally serving me papers filled with these ridiculously inflated numbers.

In turn, for my part, I've come to the realization that I will never have a weight I'm going to be proud of, or that even looks nice on a page. I will never weigh 115 pounds, 120 pounds, or even 125, which for some reason has always been ingrained in me as what adult women—or at least adult women mannequins—should weigh (in the same 1960s way, I suppose, that one's dinner table should be set with folded cloth napkins or that your purse should match your shoes).

I don't even weigh what it says on my driver's license: 137. I'm going to guesstimate I'm maybe ten pounds heavier than that, which I consider essentially identical, given the vagaries of wildly differently calibrated scales and water retention. Even when I was eighteen and first got my driver's license, 137 was a random dart throw, and to be even anywhere close to that, three decades later, I think is absolutely amazing.

Plus I was pregnant twice, and when you join that community, there is this whole galaxy of new numbers to obsess over (and to be competitive about): "That's right—I'm already twenty-four-and-a-half weeks pregnant." "Going to the hospital, I was dilated six centimeters and was over 70 percent effaced, but I still bravely said no epidural." "You were able to pump just three ounces of milk this morning? Jeez, if I don't pump at least ten, I feel like these are going to burst—!" That said (and I don't want to be harsh), I believe that when you are twenty pounds over the weight listed on your driver's license, police officers should be able to pull you over and give you a ticket. Thirty pounds over, this is false representation, and an actual violation; it's like failing to report a concealed weapon or a third leg. You may as well put down that you're the opposite gender or an entirely different species of mammal. Forty pounds over, and you should be immediately deported.

I am kidding, of course. Just a little. To tell you the truth, I have no idea exactly what I weigh these days, as I no longer own a bathroom scale. I banished it a few years ago as a conscious midlife protest against my post-boomer generation—that group of women whose chief contribution to the culture, as Judith Warner suggested in *Perfect Madness*—was arguably anorexia. I'm taking back the night, ladies. That's right, I'm lifting up my Hadassah arms and chanting, "My fat body, my fat self!"

Not that I'm remotely what a team of medical judges could call fat. Even though I'm five foot eight—well, -ish. True, I have bad posture and am shrinking—probably even five foot seven is a stretch. Anyway, even though I'm taller than the average American woman (five foot four), I'm sure I must weigh less than the average American woman (162.9 pounds). Just in case, though, to hold myself in check, I keep a couple of pairs of jeans on the floor of my closet like loaded guns that I eye warily, knowing that at any moment I could disturb my equilibrium by trying to pull them on. I don't try to pull them on, ever, but the threat is there.

Anyway, I'm not too worried because I've cobbled together a pretty reliable weight-control regimen based on my four-decade survival of Pritikin (briefly), Atkins, the Zone Diet, South Beach, and even the marvelous seventies diet Ed McMahon espoused called "martinis and whipped cream" (where you can have all the steak, butter, and gin you want,

but no carb-filled carrots). Of course, now, thanks to my rigorous training, I can have carbs, too, in moderation (cue light
wrist slap).

The secret to getting things back on track (if they've gotten off) is to eat just one meal a day. How I do it (when I am
doing it) is to ingest nothing but coffee (with milk) starting
from the time I get up in the morning until the clock reaches
the magical number 5. (Am I sometimes tempted to sleep till
noon to shrink the window until cocktail hour? Sure.) At 5:00
P.M., I slowly and mindfully break my fast, although as you
can imagine I'm pretty hungry by 5:00, so before dinner along
with wine and some artisanal slicings of cheeses, I may enjoy
some olives and two or three chunks of salami and just a bit of
sourdough baguette (it is eyed very warily and very sternly as
judicious pieces are ripped off).

Meanwhile, if I'm going to take a brush to my own canvas
here, and begin idly sketching across the white space, I think of
my weight as being an entity that generally exists in the 140s,
within which 142 feels trim-ish (really, I'd like to weigh 138,
but at this point I'm only going to get there via a light bout of
hepatitis), 145 is profoundly depressing, and a terrifying reading of 147.9 (I used to have a digital scale that measured tenths
of a pound) is practically a reason to leap off a bridge, although
clearly the gigantic cannonball when I hit the water may well
cause cataclysmic local flooding reminiscent of an action movie
by Jerry Bruckheimer.

Because for me the spectrum from nirvana to cataclysm
exists within a ten-pound range, as opposed to Mr. Y's more
grandiose fifty-pound spread, I could never do what he did

at the eco-spa, aka leap onto a scale fully clothed right in the middle of a huge dinner.

Because I myself am very careful and superstitious about when, how, and why I choose to step onto a scale. I would like some lead time first—at least two weeks—to fast and pray and prepare myself. Possibly some somber journaling would be involved, past-life Reiki sessions with a Buddhist nun, and/or a forty-eight-hour silent retreat. I want to be mindful about my intentions regarding the spiritual journey I intend to go on vis-à-vis seeing a dreaded actual number (absolution? redemption? punishment?).

I would like to perform the act first thing in the morning, in the darkness of dawn, say, before ingesting any solids or liquids or even air. To this end, preparation may be required: several preliminary trips to the bathroom to ensure total drainage, careful drying of hair (if a shower is taken, which I think sometimes adds weight, dewy moisture), the removing of a gold chain around my neck or other such poundage-increasing items such as a hair scrunchie or ring.

Also I think, as with the high jump, one's scale work benefits from a careful and well-thought-out physical approach, from the left, from the right, straight on, counterclockwise, a few small steps and then one leap, or perhaps many long steps and then sort of gingerly oozing onto it so as not to wake the monster waiting below. There may also be consideration as to how the scale is positioned à la north, south, east, and west because of magnetic polarities.

· · ·

THAT SAID, I have been working out hard now for almost five weeks, so I'm quite curious about the amazing metrics of my new rock-star body.

Because of my new musculature, including my greatly strengthened lats, it's hard to tell from my clothing, which is not terribly loose, how much weight I've dropped. I am thinking this is a time when the only way you can measure concrete results is to track your actual weight loss.

So I exhale deeply to get all the air out of my lungs, I step onto the locker-room scale—it's one of those old-school Detectos—and move the bottom weight to the left as I customarily do, to 100, causing the top arm immediately to seesaw up with its usual jailhouse-door-slamming sound. With a vague, breezy sweeping motion I slide the little weight to the right, through the twenties, thirties, forties, and . . . and . . . and . . . ? The weight is all the way to the right; if it went any farther it would actually fall off the Detecto—

And the top arm doesn't budge.

For a moment, as if in a paralyzingly complex high-school lab experiment, I literally can't process what I'm seeing. If the little weight is all the way over and the top arm doesn't budge from where it's slammed all the way up . . . ?

In dawning horror, I do something I've never done before. After sliding the little weight back to the left again, in slow motion, like a whipped dog I chunk the bottom weight from 100 to 150. Still the top arm remains grimly affixed, metal on metal. After cautiously pushing the little weight to the right, with fussy, feathery, erratic motions akin to blowing a child's fragile sailboat across a lake, when the little weight hits 7½ or even possibly 8 (but I think what I'm going to call it is 7½), the top arm finally relents and wobblingly floats down. A hair.

By my calculations—and I could be wrong—the scale reads . . .

What is it—207½? 302½? No, no, no.

What?

157½.

I must hack off a limb immediately.

THE CULPRIT can't be my failure to exercise, given my Kettlebelling so frenetically and all those reverse Kegels.

It can't be my eating habits, which are—essentially—the same. The exception is that some carbs—like rye toast, for Pete's sake, a single slice of rye toast!—have been allowed. As per my trainer's advice!

But egad, the list of things I haven't eaten: pizza, birthday cake, Chinese food—my God, Chinese food is the most fattening stuff on the planet! Even with Mexican food you may see a piece of lettuce somewhere, and with Italian food you may see an actual tomato. Chinese food has no unmolested vegetable. Chinese food is like the baccarat table. If you're even going to set foot in a Chinese restaurant, it's like a five-thousand-calorie minimum ("Oh, and have you had the ten-thousand-calorie shrimp?").

For a wild moment I consider blaming it on the fact that half the TVs at Equinox are increasingly turned to the Food Network. Bobby Flay, Giada, Big Daddy. Everyone is melting butter, grating Parmesan, sloshing in olive oil, dicing pancetta.

The Barefoot Contessa practically cannot get into her summery backyard picnic tent. Did you see that episode where, holding a fudge brownie crowned with vanilla-bean gelato, she actually capsized backward into that tent?

The point being, unless I am prepared to refinance for thirty years fixed at a 10 percent higher weight, things are going to have to change. Really change.

The culprit must be menopause.

So I turn to my stack of menopause books. Wasn't there a special menopause diet book? Okay. Here it is: *Menopause Reset!: Reverse Weight Gain, Speed Fat Loss, and Get Your Body Back in 3 Simple Steps.*

Game on! Pilot pen out.

Menopause Reset! promises—thank God—a nutritional miracle cure for that mysterious spare beach floaty that arrives after forty. *Menopause Reset!* contains some startling, amazing information, all of which is new to me. To wit: When a forty-something woman begins to notice weight gain, her first instinct might be to panic and to start denying herself. But no! Wrong! Things have changed! Your metabolism is now so slow that even if you literally fast, your body will go into such a hysterical shutdown "I am starving!" mode that the weight will continue to fly on. I still remain bewildered that Demi Moore, while depressed about Ashton Kutcher, drank champagne from morning to night and continued to become ever more skeletal (which I know thanks to Equinox TV). Champagne is carbs! It's as though Demi Moore loses weight and I put her weight on, via some kind of Stephen Hawking–type wormhole.

The secret, then, is to eat many tiny meals constantly, like

every two hours. But alas, in the horrible new metrics of midlife, each of the following (what the—?!) constitutes a *meal*:

MEAL NO. 1 (8 A.M.):
2 tsp. nonfat yogurt

MEAL NO. 2 (10 A.M.):
3 almonds (unsalted)

MEAL NO. 3 (12 P.M.):
2 oz. low-fat barley soufflé (see Appendix D)

MEAL NO. 4 (2 P.M.):
small bell pepper
1 tsp. flaxseed

Eaugh! There is no help for it but to go to the pile of books
in the garage and pull out my old tried-and-true *Zone Diet*, by
Dr. Barry Sears.

Because I know dining at home will not be harmonious if
I face a lean chicken breast while Mr. Y tucks into a massive
tureen of cheesy lasagna, I request that Mr. Y try it—or some
form of it—with me.

"A diet?" he asks warily. "What kind of diet is it?"

"It's not too punishing," I say. "It's mostly about cutting out
starches like rice and bread."

"Oh!" he said. "Then I'm fine. Look at this breakfast—
totally healthy." He is stirring honey into some strawberry
yogurt, into which he has mashed a banana.

"We-e-e-elll," I say. "It's just that—"

"What?" he stops. "It's low-fat yogurt. Does it have to be nonfat?"

"No, no, no, honey," I say. "I have to double-check, but I'm pretty sure a banana is off the glycemic index. And honey. And strawberry yogurt because the fruit has carbs. There is just this weird list of, like, carrots and bananas and butternut squash that are glycemically verboten."

Mr. Y's stirring movements become jerky with barely contained rage. "What?" he snarls. "Give me that book!"

He returns an hour later. He admits, to his own surprise, to being very impressed with all the science involved, including a lengthy section parsing glycemic indexes that I myself have never in my life been able to get through.

Game on!

WE ARE off to our local Whole Foods. Adjacent to the death star of the Equinox, ours is the largest Whole Foods west of the Mississippi, with two escalators and its own hemp clothing boutique.

The bins of quinoa beckon. The wheatgrass juicer hums.

We push our middle-aged noses eagerly forward into the organucopia.

"Omega-3-enhanced flax!" Mr. Y exclaims.

"Nonfat Swiss cheese!" I cry out.

"Tofu smart wings!" he says in awe.

"OMG," I breathe. "Look at this! Here it is, finally—zero-calorie, zero-carb noodles!"

This appears to me to be a giant breakthrough in Western civilization.

I mean, after literally decades of dieting, I do happen to know that whatever diet you're on, be it Cave Man or South Beach or Weight Watchers or Zone or even Ed McMahon's "martinis and whipped cream" diet, you can't eat pasta. Pasta is consistently out. And I love pasta.

But if we can split the atom now *and* enjoy carbohydrate- and even calorie-free pasta? Weighing a mean and lean 125 pounds? This will be almost too easy!

We cart home all our amazing treasures. Thanks to modern technology, Cajun seasoning, and a chain of mysterious Whole Foods mini-agribusinesses, we can now start building our own entire, separate, gastronomic zero-carb Shadow Kingdom empire.

I lay out my sassy new collection of nonfat cheeses. There is nonfat Swiss and nonfat cheddar and nonfat pepperjack and something arrestingly called nonfat Mexican Blend. I find that, if you squint your left eye a little when you bite into it, it does taste pretty cheesy. Kinda. Sure, to be fair this cheese does not melt—one hour in the oven and it looks less melted than vaguely perturbed, as if it would like to break out into a sweat but it can't, because of the Botox.

But no matter. Cheese! We're eatin' cheese!

And it's not only cheese. How about some nummy mashed potatoes? Okay, it's actually pureed cauliflower with just a plop of nonfat ricotta. And some nonfat Greek yogurt. But still virtually the same.

Mr. Y comes up with his own innovations. With the careful

precision of a surgeon, he takes some tofu-based smart wings, towels off the nasty red sauce, and combines them with fairly thinly sliced portobello mushrooms. Mix it all with Greek yogurt, and you've got something that approaches beef Stroganoff! All this goodness goes on a hillock of shirataki mushroom noodles—just twenty-five calories, people: twenty-five!

It is true that these zero-calorie noodles, when heated, exude a liquid that smells fishy, and that they are oddly springy in texture. Sauce doesn't adhere but rather slips and sluices off, as though the noodles—like frightened amphibians with sperm tails twitching—are trying to swim away.

Who cares if witty people like Merrill Markoe feel that these "noodles" taste like "heavy water"? Or if the Pulitzer Prize–winning food critic, Jonathan Gold, says about shirataki: "That's why the Japanese call it the devil's foot jelly"?

I say fine. As long as it's not a fat foot.

MR. Y and I believe we are geniuses. We have discovered El Dorado. We have become one of those couples who tell everyone about their amazing diet—the delicious innovative meals we are making, and how we are never hungry. Mr. Y is dreaming of inventing a pizza crust out of zero-carb seitan—if you don't know what seitan is, walk away. We are going to write a cookbook! We are going to build an app! We are going to be zillionaires!

Herewith, in handy tear-out format, is a short list from our new miracle cookbook:

Pastaless Lasagna! (It's done with eggplant)

Meatless Beef Stroganoff! (It's done with tofu chicken
   wings)

Mashed Faux-tatoes! (It's all about pureed cauliflower,
   my friends, all about pureed cauliflower)

Sans-Souci Asian Noodles! (Never mind if they are
   made of wheat flour and algae and taste like a
   foot—throw on some basil and mint leaves)

Double Down My Deviled Eggs! (It's all about pureed
   cauliflower, my friends, and mustard and scallions
   and then again pureed cauliflower)

Holy Christ! This 30-Calorie Portobello Mushroom
   with Nonfat Feta Cheese and Capers Is So Damned
   Filling I Literally Never Want to Eat Food Again,
   and I Mean It! (No further explanation needed)

Egg-White Omelet with Scallions AGAIN?! It's
   Christmas!

Deviled Egg–Like Things—did I say this already?

Sort of an Omelet!

We begin to notice now how we are starting to use a dollop of Greek yogurt as a garnish for everything. I lotion it into my heels, I rub some into scratches in our wooden floors, I put some into the choleric Volvo—and it has never run better!

A WONDERFUL thing occurs. I am fat-friended! By Isabel, busily improving our lives via computer once again. Yes, the missive is rather generic in tone—"Hello Sandra, I'm using Lose It!, a free Web site to help me lose weight. I'd like to add you as a friend so we can see each other's progress using Lose It! Once you set up your free account, you can start using Lose It! too!" Yes, I know it is suggesting that I am fat. But I have been friended by someone my own age! Fat-friended but friended nonetheless! Maybe this social networking thing has an upside after all.

Loseit.com turns out to be this handy free Web site where you can track your weight, calorie consumption, and amount of time spent exercising until that glorious moment 4 or 16 or 47 or 112 weeks later when you reach your goal weight.

Because fat friends can constantly check one another's pages, they can keep one another accountable for what they eat. Nice! Here is a brand-new midlife pick-me-up. Put it right up there with refinancing (and hey, where's my digital pedometer?)! I go on loseit.com immediately, so eager am I to log my breakfast.

In case you have not joined the magical world of fat friends and hence somehow missed my posting, let me review. Two Thursdays ago, around 10:17 A.M., I had one-third of a cup of nonfat Greek yogurt, okay? A half of a small Gala apple cut into it, and, yes, people, because I know it's good for you, although I don't remember why, a tablespoon of flaxseed. For a total—*bing!* loseit.com instantly totaled it up for me—of 133 calories.

You have to admit, a pretty impressive breakfast. I thought it looked pretty great on the page. I hated to add anything to my entry. So I didn't.

Then came the afternoon, at which point I was understandably ravenous, and I was running a little late to pick the kids up, so I stopped logging food as there would have been just too much typing and I was feeling so weak . . .

"Well, have you looked at *my* page?" Isabel asks in wonderment. "For breakfast, slice of wheat toast, egg whites, tomatoes. For lunch, nonfat cottage cheese, small spinach salad, half a tangerine. For dinner, one cup of low-fat vegetarian chili with side of steamed broccoli, but then, after dinner, whoops! I lost it and did like three shots of Jack Daniel's! And they were pretty big shots that waitress was pouring. I mean, measured with my thumb? They looked like at least three and a half or four ounces. Loseit.com calculated that all comes out to about four thousand calories!"

"Liquor counts?" I ask in horror. "What other pleasure is left to us in an empty world, full of nonfat Greek yogurt and flax?"

Isabel claims that, after age forty-five, if you keep drinking wine with dinner, it's just going to be an extra seven pounds, no matter what. She cites her friend Janelle, who devotes a full half of her daily Weight Watchers points to pinot grigio.

To which I retort that perhaps we fat friends can all just agree to carry the extra seven pounds, and we should start an online support group.

"And call it what?" Isabel says. "Drunk fat friends dot com?"

I'M READY for my next weigh-in.

I have eschewed cheese, eggs, ice cream, chocolate. Bread is—toast!

Which should be a bumper sticker: BREAD—TOAST.

After a hard workout with Stef, I have just steam-roomed for ten minutes—that's good for losing at least a pound. I've had a very thorough shower—didn't get the hair wet, which I believe, even if you towel it out, can add half a pound. I have shaved off everything except the hair on my head and left the eyebrows, at least some of the eyebrows. I have removed my necklace. And then very gingerly—very quietly—I approach the Detecto from the right, which I believe is its lucky side.

What the—?

I have actually gained another two pounds!

I have been weight training twice a week, doing cardio another four days of the week, and eating nonfat cheese and noodles that are literally zero calories.

I have become this astonishing creature who makes fat out of air!

The Shit Hits the Fan

BUT NOW EVERYTHING REALLY goes to hell. As if getting through the day isn't challenging enough, it is at this point that I lose it completely. It is at this point that a major break occurs. It is the break that must come, finally and inevitably, with Mr. Y. I've been living for too long in a dream world, I've been ignoring the fact that, now that the honeymoon phase is over, my relationship with Mr. Y is getting more and more broken, even useless. Our life together makes less and less sense. Less an asset than a drain, Mr. Y is becoming yet another thing I am caretaking, along with my house, my children, my father, and all these other oversize items sitting around my space, waiting for me to run them or to fix them or to have them cleaned.

A major change has to occur, and it has to occur immediately. And no, I am not just thinking this because I am hungry, tired, irritated, and bloated all at once. Although that certainly is true. I feel in a constant low-level rage every single day. Why?

Well, it is not just that I have been on such a strict Zone regime I have been taking low-fat salad dressing and diluting it further with rice vinegar to get the fat grams from four to two, or that I have counted the carbs in ketchup. (Potential epitaph for tombstone: I HAVE COUNTED THE CARBS IN KETCHUP.)

It is not just that I have been working out five mornings a week, even biking to the gym sometimes, then returning to my computer to work on this big baggy think piece on women in politics that's sort of killing me, while hydrating all day with water and green tea.

It is not even the fact, really, that after almost three months, after all this mindful application, I have actually gained two pounds while Mr. Y has lost—no kidding—twenty-three. And he feels terrific. How is this possible? As opposed to me, Mr. Y has allowed himself the occasional bagel and chocolate bar and has even begun taking non-Zone lunch meetings with some of his old theater buddies. ("I'm not going to lie—I had pad thai. And spring rolls. And a beer.") Increasingly also, instead of the gym, there is an afternoon of golf at the local community course, which as far as I can tell, when done with a golf cart counts as neither weight training nor cardio.

Oh no. All these things I might have borne, but then Mr. Y went one step too far. Certainly, I was going on a bit long about the unfairness of it all, saying, "I can't believe that with how little I eat, and how much I exercise, I can't actually move the needle any way but up!"

MENOPAUSE TIP (FOR MEN)

Dear Men,

Note that if a female close to you utters something like the above sentence, appropriate responses include:

"Oh honey, it *is* unfair! Damned unfair! Fuck the world! Scheisse!"

"I think you could gain another twenty and actually start to look normal—why are you trying to hang on to this skeletal weight? I'm seeing collarbones!" (Note: Say this whether or not it is actually true.)

"Darling—I can't bear to see you suffer. I threw away the scale and made you a martini." (Or similar.)

What you should not say is what Mr. Y said on this day, aka: "I know you say that you work out every day, honey, but maybe it's *how* you work out. Fabrizio says you have to really intensify your cardio in order to burn fat. Once you get your heart rate up to 145 it really has to stay there. For as long as 20–30 continuous minutes. To really score that maximum burn." He may also have foolishly said: "I think that's why I can eat a bagel and still lose weight. It's true I don't work out as often as you do, but when I do I really go for it."

This all comes, for me, on top of this three-thousand-word think piece that is killing me and a clutch of women's magazine pieces that all have the same deadline, which will bring in a good amount of sorely needed income but upon which I do really need to mentally focus and concentrate.

. . .

WHILE HURTLING—late—along the 101 as usual to pick up my kids, I see a fish-without-a-bicycle-type bumper sticker that says: "MENopause MENstrual cramps MENtal illness. It all begins with men." And that's when my slow burn begins to fan into flame.

There is something about a recent conversation we've had that is gnawing at me.

Mr. Y and I are generally so in tune with each other we're like, I don't know, twin currents of a warm stream flowing together. My belief is that Mr. Y is basically a fair person who can be reasoned with. I feel he really listens to me and is sensitive to my feelings. But I feel he has not been so in this particular case. The evidence will demonstrate it.

"I just feel like you committed to this diet-and-exercise program to help us both out, which is clearly harder for me than it is for you. I'm really frustrated with how bloated I am—how I'm carrying this extra trunk around my waist—which makes more stress. And now this other menopause book is recommending I add baby aspirin, which they say helps stem inflammation—I mean, all these weight loss tips are quite a lot to keep track of! I really just have to stay on this. I've got a lot of stress on my plate, and I really could use your help!"

"What?" he says, from behind his *New York Times*. "What are you saying, exactly?"

"I'm saying just because I'm miserable doesn't mean you

have to be miserable. At the same time, I think it's inconsiderate to report all the non-Zone stuff you're always having for lunch with Sam and Wilson or whomever."

"You asked me specifically to tell you."

"Well, I didn't know you were having pad thai and spring rolls and beer!"

"You want me to lie?"

"Jeez, I guess! I had no idea you were going to go that far off the ranch. I guess if you're planning to make that choice, just do it and don't tell me."

Mr. Y sighs, lowers his paper, and takes off his reading glasses.

"Oh, but this is not just about food."

"Of course it is!"

"I can't believe you're getting this hung up about food."

My voice cracks. I feel teary at the unfairness of it. "You don't believe it because you just don't know how hard it is!"

"You're taking this—"

"Oh! It's like when someone borrows money from a friend, they don't repay it, the friend gets mad, and then the borrower says, 'Oh, but this is not about the money, it's about something else'? No, no, it's about the money! I mean the food!"

He is gesturing with his glasses now.

"No, I think it's the fact that I'm going to be producing this show."

"What show?" I am truly surprised. I thought his meetings were all about golf and breezily high-carb lunches.

"I flagged this a few weeks ago, but apparently you forgot.

Jam City is coming back into town. My coproducers and I have finally put the package together, and we're going to do this six-week run."

"What?"

"That's what I said," he says, a bit defiantly.

"I'm . . . confused," I say. "I thought you gave that all up. And with *Jam City*, which was that hip-hop show, right? I thought you hated those producers. You told me they were lame. It's why you didn't want to do that sort of work anymore. For the time you put into those shows and for what you tend to net, it's like minimum wage!"

His cheeks flush red. His face darkens. He narrows his eyes, looks out the window. "Whatever you think, it's a show I've been involved with for a long time, and I don't recall ever saying I was giving up my career in theater."

"Well actually you did!" I say. "Remember on the drive back from Burning Man? When we said we were done with all the stress of life and we were just going to manage and continue to develop the business streams we've already built up over ten years—the income and maybe royalties from my speeches, shows, books, and teaching while traveling and cooking and relaxing, as the kids got older? You said you were done with theater. You were over it. That was the deal! It was very explicit."

"I said no such thing! You're hallucinating!"

I feel my throat closing due to the unfairness of it, and due to the apparent gaps in his surprisingly faulty memory. But a tunnel of white is opening, before me—it is a truth channel, and I feel I have to express myself: "Honey, I told you I have already been married to a person who continually disappeared into his work. The point was that you wouldn't disappear into your work! I'd already been abandoned for show business once before!"

He is almost shouting by now: "Oh please! There is literally no resemblance between Mr. X and myself! I can't even believe you would make that connection. I can't believe my ears! It's absurd! It's a six-week run, for crying out loud!"

"But you know what show schedules are like! It's six nights a week! Load-in days go from 10:00 A.M. to midnight!"

"I'm not general managing. I don't have to be there every night," he says unconvincingly.

"But you will!" I flash out. "I know how you are!"

"Well, it's my life!"

I can't believe it.

"But what about me? Who's going to help me?" I shrill.

"You?" he flashes back. "Why is it always about you? It's like you're jealous if I even express interest in anyone else's project! You can't even be bothered to pay attention."

Tears sting my eyes. This is hurtful, if possibly true, but it is also beside the point. "It's just that I make so much more money than you do," I wail, "and I need help, and this was the arrangement!"

His eyes narrow.

"Well, you know what, I've been in theater thirty years. I've had a career long before I started"—he enunciates the words precisely—"holding your fanny pack."

I am hyperventilating. I look at Mr. Y's face, once handsome and loving but now a dead-eyed mask . . . and I feel my spirit recede, wash out and away like the tide. My dad was a rager, and when he used to go off in the evenings at my mother when I was a child I would simply shut down. Mr. X and I had a stable twenty-year relationship because we literally never fought. If we began to get into conflict, Mr. X would say, "Never mind. Let's forget it. It's not worth fighting over." Perhaps we ended up living parallel lives, but perhaps there's something to be said for that.

I spend that night in Sally's bedroom. Silence falls over the house.

In the morning, Mr. Y brings me coffee and does his cheerful WASP "Let's try again, shall we?" gesture where he punches me lightly in the arm and grins ruefully. Because our natural inclination is to be easy with each other, Mr. Y and I take deep breaths, hug, and apologize.

"I didn't mean to insult your profession and apologize if I came off as an ass," I say.

"Look, I've thought it over and I can structure this deal a different way if it will cause that much upset," he says.

But from long experience with men and their work, I realize if I insist that he doesn't do this work exactly the way he wants, he will only resent me, and more than anything I do not want to be hated.

It's only six weeks. It's good to have projects, after all. And the money, while not giant, will help.

I will get through this. I will be a good person about this. I will develop a sense of humor.

. . .

BUT AS the weeks pass, frustrations and irritations keep bubbling up like a geyser.

Now that we've been cohabiting for two years, Mr. Y and I have drifted at home into a T-shirt-and-sweatpants thing (which has long been my uniform, but I was surprised to discover that the usually natty Mr. Y had T-shirts and sweatpants as well). And that was fine. But now of course, each morning, after reading the *New York Times* for an hour, he showers, shaves, and selects a new tie and jacket before sailing out of the house with unrestrained joy. He even dresses to the nines when there aren't any meetings. I see him standing before his closet comparing ties, one against another. And none of it's for me.

With my Shanghai abacus, next come the cost-benefit analyses. I can't stop running the abacus—it is practically an internal physical organ, like my heart or my liver. Mr. Y is spending more and more hours (I keep count) at a venue that's an hour each way with traffic. The gas and the dry-cleaning alone are a couple of hundred bucks a month. And of course, as events would have it, not much of the money he makes (he won't tell me how much) flows into our household. Up in the Bay Area, his twenty-six-year-old son is hard at work finishing his first novel, which he really believes in, and so just for a few months Mr. Y is helping him out. A fair bit. I can't help recalling that when I myself was the exact same age—twenty-six—and I was in a similar situation with Mr. X, myself trying to write, he refused to pay my rent for me (as he had for his ex; besides, he pointed out, no one ever had for him) and I had to get a temp job. It was an excellent experience, I learned to be more disciplined, and all was well. But no, young people today are fragile, San Francisco is expensive, and times are different.

Everywhere you look in our relationship, there are tributaries upon tributaries of conflict, lighting up everywhere like a troubled PET scan.

Meanwhile, our household is sliding into total disarray, which, due to having to write almost a thesis-load of magazine pieces to pay all our bills, I'm powerless to stop. It is true that it's not his fault that Charter cable has temporarily cut off our Internet. This is apparently due to the fact that, thanks to the three cheapo old Toshiba laptops that I have, which my daughters peck away at like rabies-infected raccoons when I'm on deadline and scold them, our house is radiating—just seeping, suppurating—so much spam it is actually fritzing out other Wi-Fi connections on our block. We are sending out so much Moshi Monster spam, it's like we have Internet lice.

That said—as he darts in and out of our home, backing out of the driveway with a fresh travel mug, babbling into his headphones—like sand dunes, laundry is piling up, dishes choke the sink, newspapers and magazines swirl on every chair, and, perhaps most regrettably, on our balcony bowls overflow with ash from his cigarettes (one of the nasty habits he allows himself when he is in "show mode").

It is starting to feel less like a house with rooms and cabinets and more like a field of nests, and many of them are his nests.

Our home is such, it seems, that every utilitarian object is displayed and visible except for the one item you are looking for (scissors, keys, can opener), and now—pull up the next cue—

here come the ants. That's right—due to a sudden unseasonal heat, the earth has vomited forth ants from every corner. There are ants in the kitchen, ants in the girls' rooms, ants in the tub, even—and what kind of metaphor is this?—ants on my computer. There are literally ants on my computer keyboard. It's like something out of *Le Chien Andalou*. All I am missing are melting clocks and maybe a razor across a leaking eyeball.

But as Mr. Y points out, being more impressively Zen than myself, he is not bothered by ants, which are natural harmless creatures that will go away on their own schedule when the weather changes. Too, my nervous habit of agitatedly spraying Windex at the ants (George12! George12! George12!) is essentially poisoning us, by inadvertantly misting things like our dishes, utensils, and fruit with window cleaner. All this may be technically true, but in the meantime I am brushing ants off my computer, and every time the girls enter the house (coming from their dad's house, where there are no ants; Sally's flat pronouncement: "Dad says to get rid of ants you have to put food away") and see the delicate shimmering trails, they utter piercing shrieks in that particular tween two-octaves-above-middle-C register that makes my bone marrow shiver. While all the time I am trying to mentally focus and concentrate in order to pay our mortgage (which includes property tax). And what about the home insurance? Did we pay the home insurance? That is Mr. Y's job, and they are claiming we are late.

When I call him at work—where I can hear conversation and laughter in the background ("The costumes just came—oh my God!")—Mr. Y keeps saying that everything will be fine, this is not a crisis, all of it is manageable. What I should try to bring down is my stress level, and that I can do by breathing . . .

Which is not a good dynamic between us. The more I come under stress, the more New Agey he goes, and the more his "advice" backfires. To wit:

1. Advice: If I just let go of my negative catastrophic thought patterns, I will be able to get rid of my continuing insomnia and sleep easily through the night as he does. Result: I continue to lie awake every night with my mind racing as usual, but now I also berate myself for being a bad sleeper.

2. Advice: If I say I'm feeling sad or stressed, he gently parries with the wisdom that we choose all our moods, the (supposedly) good news being that we actually have power over our own minds. Result: This of course simply makes me feel more anxious, because now instead of just being blue I am a person who makes self-destructive choices ("Oh great—and now I am going mad") and who has lost all perception of reality (because I have no memory of actually "choosing" the bad mood).

3. Advice: To bring myself more peace, I should begin meditation. He gives me CDs from Eckhart Tolle to listen to in my car. They were given to him by one of his partners on *Jam City*. The other day they were all talking about mindfulness and controlling one's emotions, and they all agreed these were really important things.

Sample Tolle passage: "Resistance is an inner contraction, a hardening of the shell of the ego. You are closed. Whatever action you take in a state of inner resistance (which we could also call negativity) will create more outer resistance, and the universe will not be on your side; life will not be helpful." Result: I want to punch him *and* Eckhart Tolle in the face. "Life will not be helpful"? "Nor will your male partner," I should add.

The horrible truth is that, aside from the nests, when Mr. Y is at his job and my kids are with Mr. X, I feel terribly lonely in my big clattering house. Sometimes all I can think of to get through the day is draw a number line from 8:00 A.M. to 8:00 P.M. and shakily shade my progress to the evening in half-hour intervals. (My own version of *Fifty Shades of Grey*.) When he comes home fifteen minutes later than usual ("I got caught in this conversation about the ticketing—") I am outraged.

Dinnertime has gone from dreadful to nightmarish. When the girls are in, I just feed them at 5:00 as I used to. Which in a way is a blessing.

When the girls are away, Mr. Y and I try for increasingly rare "date nights" (oh my gosh—has it come to this now, date night?). I cook dinner now and set the table for us both, being that he is now not the Ethel to my Lucy but rather the Lucy to my Ethel. (I have also started to take in his dry cleaning for him because time is so short on his days off I do not want him to consume all his free time with errands.) Due to his schedule, we often eat at strange late hours, but it's the best we can do.

So here we are, shakily, putting one candle in a candlestick, can't find the other.

I make the mistake of asking: "How was your day?" He makes the mistake of nattering on about the play, and as I watch his mouth move, I feel an itchy trigger finger and think those awful words only a woman who needs a man neither to support her nor to be a father to her children can think: How long until I vote you off the island?

So while I and the house are being neglected, where has his customary WASP love and service gone? Into the hapless cast of *Jam City*. I can hear Mr. Y delivering his special personal care on the phone (which he picks up at all hours of the day or night): "Absolutely. I am completely available. Call me anytime." I notice him putting an old floor lamp from our garage into his car. What the—? He explains that one of the out-of-town dancers, SpookyZ, needs a lamp for her temporary apartment, and he knew we weren't using it anyway. I see him printing out twenty résumés for the ten-year-old son of one of the actors, which is not technically his job but he offered to help out as a favor.

AT THIS moment in life, when the stories are never elegant, everything tends to go wrong at once. There is now a sad turn involving Alice, my father's little Chinese wife. It seems that her penchant for chattering Chinese at one no matter how many times one reminded her one was American was not, as we'd thought, due to her natural girlish sweetness or simply a symptom of her English skills plateauing after fifteen years.

Oddly, Alice is starting to . . . disappear. Increasingly, she is being found wandering at 2:00 A.M. on freeways in places like Torrance (fifty miles away), and is being brought home in the dead of night by police officers.

Meanwhile, forensic analysis reveals that Alice has withdrawn thirteen thousand dollars, gone to a bank in Chinatown, and purchased a useless universal life-insurance policy, an event she cannot recall. Clearly Alice is getting confused. But the situation is more acute than that. Alice is now even starting to disturb the tenants—the tenants! She is waving butcher knives at them, hurling their things into the street, setting fires in the backyard (Malibu is brushfire country). She is also starting to hit my father, leaving him bruised and bleeding.

I learn this last bit via the Malibu police, whom my father called because Alice was hitting him—not to have her arrested but, as my dad says, just to "scare" her. To evade capture, Alice ran away with a duffel bag stuffed with their passports, marriage certificate, immigration papers, and two small, tightly packed envelopes, one with exactly thirteen crisp one-dollar bills inside it and another with a Keystone Kops–type mélange of Chinese money, Turkish money, and . . . as I said ruefully, upon discovery, to my sister: "I didn't know Bill Nye the Science Guy *had* his own currency." When I gave Alice the bag (returned by the police), she accused me of stealing two thousand dollars from it.

In short, a doctor's visit confirms that Alice's once-quaint-seeming disconnects are actually symptoms of deepening dementia, the crows that are now coming to roost. Which is to say that instead of being my dad's twenty-years-younger insurance policy, it is now a relatively young seventy-two-year-old Alice who requires full-time care, at six thousand dollars a month, and she could live—what?—another twenty years? At that rate she will go through all his money, and then Kaitlin and I will have to begin to pay.

We've just seen this happen with Patty, a longtime family friend of ours. Patty had just gone through a devastating experience with her mother, Sabine, who lived until ninety-eight—ninety-eight! By the end of Sabine's life, the last ten years of which she had spent in various states of dementia, the family was totally destroyed. Even though they had secured long-term-care insurance early on, due to various (Medicare? Medicaid? Medi-Cal?) complications (involving shoring up? spending down? who could follow it?), the care of Patty's mother ended up costing the family the staggering amount of almost six hundred thousand dollars. Patty cut her work to half-time to oversee the constantly shifting emergency modes of her mother's care, while gradually annexing more and more of her and her husband's savings to pay for it. This in turn financially impacted her children's choices of college, setting off a range of tortuous family dynamics.

Over this time it seems Patty herself has aged thirty years. Though her mother had a relatively benign disease (I visited Sabine once in her convalescent home and, albeit probably medicated, she seemed waxy and distant but calm), by contrast Patty has had a viral one. Before one's eyes, you could watch forty-something Patty herself changing into an old person. Under the shadow of her mother's decline, she descended into the frowse of the full-time caregiver, she whose tireless efforts no one else understands. The hair frizzed and grayed; her resting expression changed: the eyebrows went helpless; the mouth sagged; the shoulders rounded and dropped. Patty even began dressing like a senior, in bulky cardigans (due to the cold hospitals) and flat almost nurselike shoes (due to long walks to the parking structures, she said, carrying multiple bags of supplies—the medicines, hot-water bottles, medical tights).

Clearly Patty—the eldest daughter—felt guilty about her mother, perhaps overly so, and she lost perspective around weighing the needs of her still-growing family against the needs of her ever-declining mother.

But Kaitlin will not make that same mistake, because Kaitlin is a brilliant manager. So she jumps into full gear to manage the Alice project. Her efforts are heroic. She is eventually able not just to switch over Alice's health insurance (for years, my father hadn't purchased her any, preferring to play the odds on her relatively young age), but to find the only assisted-living facility in California that has Mandarin-speaking caregivers. Kaitlin is able to do that after an enormous amount of research, augmented by the fact that she is both a development director and former scientist, speaks Mandarin herself, and has the laser focus of the Terminator. The facility is a relative bargain at four thousand dollars a month, given that Alice requires a private room, due to her penchants for ceaseless pacing until 4:00 A.M., putting on the clothing of her roommates, and, well, going to the bathroom in the middle of the floor and then bagging up and hiding . . . what has come out. While Alice has traveled, I have performed backup when I can, pouring a heavily medicated Alice from her wheelchair into my Volvo, or helping lift her wheelchair in a winch onto a—all hands waiting, with goggles and safety gloves and orange jumpsuits—Southwest flight. But it is never enough; my sister is doing one hundred times more than I am, and I continually fail her. Except for terse Alice emergencies, the phone lines between us lapse into icy silence. And you remember there is also my dad. As opposed to a mentally addled wife/caregiver, Dad now gets his own health professional—a forty-two-year-old Filipino male nurse named Thomas—and as a result he is suddenly receiving the best care of his life. Understand that my Dumpster-diving father is a man who can survive on things like past-its-due-date sushi and the leftovers of other people's Starbucks coffee. He has ingested bacteria for so many decades he may actually have morphed into another life-form (with a resting pulse rate of 34, I remind you). But now—hydrated, fed, washed, and laundered—weirdly, my father is roaring back with a formidable energy. Which is to say we now have a sometimes-wheelchair-bound but nonetheless always extremely active now eighty-nine-year-old who greatly enjoys getting bathed and diapered and fed ice cream and crashing UCLA science lectures and—oh, by the way . . . every day he calls me now—are you ready for this? He wants *sex*. He proudly needs only one-sixteenth of a Viagra pill for *sex*. There is some automatic Googling to find, to one's slow-blossoming horror, in-home services that use the phrase "healing hands"!

And this is merely to try to protect those around him—he has started to proposition female nurses at his doctor's office, trying to grab their breasts, begging them to touch him. Which he can't do himself, as he can barely clasp his hand around a spoon.

As Ann notes, in an e-mail exchange we have about it:

"That's disturbing not in a having-sex-with-Donald-Trump way but in the sense of carrying a corpse up a flight of stairs."

I am half tempted to hit my dad on the head with a frying pan just to calm him down, but then even I will go to jail.

It is, of a piece, heart wrenching and frustrating and terrifying and irritating and awful and thankless and hopeless and expensive—did I say expensive?

BUT IT'S the bowl of fruit, finally, that does me in.

One afternoon, I am running errands for my kids and my dad and my dad's caregiver, Thomas. (As he is the only caregiver who will stay with my father, Kaitlin and I now basically work for him. I have just completed a bout of fixing up a beater car for him and checking it and smogging it and getting it handicapped plates.) I stop in at Crate and Barrel, quite frankly, to smell some Lavender, Rose Hip, and Ylang-Ylang pillar candles. There, I've said it. I don't buy those pillar candles, I just pick them up, close my eyes, and smell them, in order to ingest a little—oh, what do you call it?—happiness.

But on the way to the wicker-basket-flanked aromatherapy section, I come upon a sight that does me in. It is a soft-lighted display of perfect tangelos in a kiln-fired celadon-hued bowl. Of all the fantasy settings of Crate and Barrel that I always laugh off (really? I'm going to sit at a desk under a silver-framed photo of Hemingway and type on this antique typewriter?), it is this sight that stops me.

I am actually stopped.

Who are the women who maintain houses whose every

room contains a bowl of beautiful seasonal fruit, fruit that is magically not rotten? It is unthinkable that, in my own house, there might be a ceramic bowl that is not full of old keys and dead AA batteries and rusty nails.

A glowing celadon bowl of perfect tangelos.

It cuts me to my heart.

Biting my lip to hold back the tears, I send Mr. Y an admittedly cryptic text: "PERFECT BOWL OF FRUIT SO NOT MY LIFE. VERY UNHAPPY ABOUT JAM CITY AND HAVOC IT IS WREAKING."

His reply is that he is sorry I am feeling badly but will be home late. We can talk about it on Monday (five days from now).

He is *so not hearing me.*

Couples Therapy Round 117

M R. Y DOES AGREE to find a hole in his busy schedule into which he can fit some couples therapy. I haven't been to couples therapy in years. It gives one pause when you realize you have lived long enough to have had couples therapy over several decades with multiple partners.

I admit that I have mixed feelings about therapy. In my experience couples therapy is typically a nice way for one person to say, "My crazy partner needs therapy." But of course the crazy partners need to be driven to therapy, otherwise they won't go because they don't think they're crazy, and then anyway on the upside you, the normal person, get the added midlife pleasure of watching a therapist in slow motion read your surprised crazy partner the riot act about what an unbelievable jerk he is.

That's the dream, anyway. Sadly, though, I have found that no matter how provably wrong one's partner is, therapists play this game where they don't take sides. Instead of simply ordering your partner to stop doing what he's doing, the therapist will just turn to one and ask: "How does that make you *feel*?"

Still, one tries, if one can, always to improve one's relationship. So here I am again, as if in a dream, sitting in another little waiting room under another row of Tibetan masks, with the little light switch flipped up. We are seeing a Beverly Hills couple's therapist with the enigmatic name of Dr. Stacey, at the suggestion, of course, of my friend Ann.

I survey my own internal landscape. The illustrative tale I used to tell about husband number one—if you'll recall—was this. After being away for a month on the road, Mr. X would step onto the porch, put his bags down, look up above him, and say, "The roof needs retiling." Because he didn't first say, "And how are you?" I like to claim that there was an emotional connection, after twenty years of cohabitation, that had gone missing.

By contrast, Mr. Y and I have plenty of emotional connection, but we also seem, more and more, to fight like dogs. His show has been extended, which is glorious but not necessarily lucrative, not yet, it has a ways to go, and he has pledged to pick up his share of the housework if not more, but it's not happening. So all our tension and strife starts to boil down into domestic affairs of the most mundane nature, which have come to represent our mutual incompatible personality differences writ large.

Dr. Stacey, a tall brunette with round glasses, a long sad face, and a knee-length maroon cardigan, regretfully flicks the light switch down and somberly greets us.

"So, Sandra," she says, smoothing her skirt as she sits. "I'm interested to hear you describe your situation."

"Well," I say. "In a nutshell I feel that Mr. Y has thrown our life out of balance by coproducing this show without really thinking it through—and our home life is really suffering."

"And how do you think he feels?" she asks gently.

I know the answer to that too!

Smartly I retort, "I would say Mr. Y, in turn, feels that he would like to pursue things he is interested in and I am too stressed out and too micromanaging of his time. What is the contract, though? I would ask. What is the contract?"

"What contract?" Mr. Y erupts. "We are partners—and we support each other in whatever we want to do in life! That's what people who love each other do! It's simple! We don't need a contract!"

"Oh but we do," I say, in a sudden deeper tone of voice.

"What do you mean?" asks Dr. Stacey quietly.

"Well, in the old days," I say, "I did the art, Mr. Y managed the art, and then when we got together, well . . ." I turn to him. "You seemed more domestic than I did, you were a better cook and into all the kitchen stuff, I paid the bills, we were in a kind of flow."

Mr. Y's mouth is in a line, and he is shaking his head.

"What do you mean, you did the art?" asks Dr. Stacey. "I need a little background."

"To be entirely candid"—I forge forward, not knowing what else to do—"during our ten-year partnership when Mr. Y was producing my one-woman shows, I was indeed, well, I'm sorry, that's what you call it—the talent. That means when you have to go onstage in one hour and perform for one hundred or six hundred people who have paid forty dollars a ticket and you have a sore throat, someone will rush out to the corner and get you two or three flavors of cough drops. It is kind of amazing. I recall the first time I saw a professionally laid-out dressing room, when I first hit the repertory theater circuit (and hence, in my modest profession, the big leagues). In the corner, your freshly dry-cleaned costume will be hung up waiting for you, wireless microphone coiled and ready, shoes polished. In front of a mirror a fresh white towel will be laid out with Alka-Selzers, Ricolas, bottled water, tea makings, a basket of crackers, a bowl of fruit, or whatever else you have requested. Everyone's job is to get what you requested."

"And you thought that would continue when you moved in with Mr. Y?"

I know this is tricky territory, but I am lulled by the facts that Dr. Stacey's expression is completely nonjudgmental and that the tone of her voice is absolutely neutral. I know we have entered that weird, beautiful therapy space where you can say things and they simply hover.

"Okay, well—as embarrassing as it is to admit, I guess some dinosaur part of my brain thought some part of this was going to continue. When we were just business partners Mr. Y would run across town to help me on a number of things, some business related, some more domestically related, particularly when Mr. X was away. He would drop everything because, I now see, I was the client. When he'd escort me around socially, which was also largely for business, I did come to think of it indeed a bit like . . . well, Jackie O and Maurice Tempelsman. There,

I've said it. But don't all working warrior-esses secretly want a chivalrous man to hold out an umbrella as we step tremulously out of Doubleday into the rain? And believe me, if you'd been there, you'd have seen that not only was Mr. Y always perfectly dressed for the role of gentleman escort, he actually seemed to get a kick out of it. 'Madame!' he'll always say, conspicuously rising from the table when a lady rises. Although of course, having lived with him for two years, I am coming to see all those elaborate WASP manners as a kind of straight-man drag, the performance that goes with the tie.'"

"A performance?!" Mr. Y exclaims. "Oh please! You're just jealous that I have anything else to do in the world! It's sick!"

"Wait," Dr. Stacey says. "Let her finish. So what did you think your lives together would be like?"

"Well, I"—this is frustrating but in a way also disturbing and interesting—"I guess I did have the idea that as my work flow became more centered on writing, we would become more of a couple like, damn it all anyway, Virginia and Leonard Woolf. If I earned the privilege by doing the work and making the money—while resisting the urge to put stones in my pockets and wade into a river—which in that sense puts female writers like me ahead of Ms. Woolf—what's wrong with that?"

Mr. Y can keep silent no longer.

"What's wrong with it is that it is demeaning to describe someone as the Ethel to your Lucy and to think of them as a kind of human golden retriever!" (Whoops—is that language he got from me?) "Look at me. I am your partner. Your partner. That means if I want to work on *Jam City*, which is my profession and which even allows me to do some recorded voice-over, which I enjoy, I'm not going to lie, you are supposed to be supportive of me in the same way I have been tireless and *happily* supportive of you all these many years! You're supposed to show the same interest in my projects as I have shown in yours!"

Mr. Y looks at me dramatically, with big moist eyes.

"How do you feel about that?" asks Dr. Stacey.

"Well," I say. "I'm weighing how I feel about that, and honestly it feels very unsexy."

"Oh my God!" he exclaims.

"What can I say? I know I shouldn't feel this way, but I wanted Maurice Tempelsman holding an umbrella in the rain! If I asked Mr. Y to drive the elephant today, he would be insulted! And that was the whole point! He was the guy who would drive the elephant! That's why I fell in love with him! That was it! Men who work are a dime a dozen! But men who will drive the elephant—"

"What elephant? I don't understand the reference," says Dr. Stacey.

"You're just a big fat diva!" Mr. Y shouts.

"Sure I'm a diva!" I shout back. "*What was your first clue?* I made my living doing one-woman shows! At this rate, I could have stuck with Mr. X, be left alone as usual, but I'd still be ahead on the home repair, which Mr. X managed very, very well! With the amount of time you put into your projects and small financial returns and the wreck the house is in, I'm essentially tolerating your hobbies!"

"You're insane, you know that?" he says in a fit of pique. "You're a complete ass. You have literally no idea what producers do! You have no respect for my profession! And you know why I spend so many hours in the theater? Maybe I like to get out of the house! Maybe it's fun! Maybe sometimes I prefer it to being with you! Look at what you've become! It's like you're a person who needs help wiping her own ass!" This is all so terrible we end up apologizing to each other, fairly quickly, our faces white and pained.

Therapists being what they are, though, Dr. Stacey finds our clash so interesting she feels—to get quickly up to speed—that she needs a separate individual session with each of us. This technically will result in even more of an overbooking problem, at least on the part of Mr. Y, and yet I remember that the therapy was my idea. If he is going to come to his senses he does probably need a lot more therapy time.

Yet I can also see that, because Mr. Y has offered to drive the girls to school on Friday morning before going to work, he will have a conflict with his individual Dr. Stacey session. So I e-mail Dr. Stacey, copying Mr. Y, reminding all that his Friday morning session will need to be moved. (This being the sort of follow-up task Mr. Y sometimes forgets.)

Dr. Stacey thanks me for my interesting e-mail, and says we'll discuss it, which surprises me, since my e-mail seemed fairly routine and uninteresting to me. And, indeed, at our next session, Dr. Stacey opens with, "So, Sandra, let's talk about your interesting e-mail. I found it interesting that you e-mailed me about Mr. Y's therapy session. Without telling him?"

"I copied him."

"Yes, but you took it upon yourself to basically reschedule his session."

She turns to Mr. Y. "Do you think Sandra has control issues?"

Mr. Y perks right up. Oh my! He has been flung such a meaty bone! He starts into a monologue. The case freezer I bought, so I can buy sixteen chicken breasts at a time at Costco and so I can freeze milk, to ensure that we never run out of milk. Or the fact that I never buy less than thirty-six rolls of toilet paper—to me, buying four or six rolls at a time is like buying none. The fact that I like everyone to be punctual for dinner, preferably at 6:00, not 8:00 or 8:30. I am not terribly tolerant of smoking, Mr. Y's unfortunate habit. When I'm on a writing deadline I cannot tolerate seeing the *New York Times* first thing in the morning because it violently jars my morning concentration. (I tend to say, "If I see all that great writing already there in the *New York Times*, it makes me think, then why does the world need me to write also?")

I am shocked at the bewildering turn the session has taken.

"The reason I sent the e-mail," I cry out, stung, "is that I knew if Mr. Y forgot, which he sometimes does, you would charge us for the full session anyway! What is the difference between taking care of business and control issues?" I ask. "What is the difference between courteously buttoning up your pants in the morning and being 'obsessively fixated on closure'?"

"Very interesting," Dr. Stacey breathes. "So . . . did you feel abandoned by your mother? Where does this anxiety come from? How old were you when you started feeling that?"

And I say, "I don't feel like talking about my mother! I want to talk about how Mr. Y and I divvy up the housework. I want to talk about the fact that I ask him to do something, he doesn't do it, I ask it again, I am the noodge, he doesn't do it, and then I finally decide to do it myself, which he takes as evidence that I am always pushing rudely forward without him when he claims that he was going to do it anyway! But *when*?"

Dr. Stacey says, more gently, "Aha. Why don't you feel like talking about your mother?"

And I say, "Dr. Stacey? I would love to talk to you about my mother for hours and hours if you and I were naked in a hot tub at a women's retreat and we were being plied with wine and hummus. I could cry for you, get into the fetal position, ruminate about our breasts—whatever. I could give you a very good performance. However, Dr. Stacey, we are paying you God knows what an hour to help us live together, which is why I *do not want to waste time on my mother who is dead* and who *does not live with us* and who *cannot help with the dishes no matter how much she may want to!*"

At which point I throw a coffee cup ("Fresh Air with Terry Gross") at the therapist.

Or at least I want to. I shove it at her but then worry about the light carpet. But believe me, my feelings are unbelievably violent. And I am—oh my God—*so* hungry.

THANK GOD the girls are going out of town with their dad on a two-week rafting trip.

I would have Mr. Y move out, but I am so sick of my own house I check into a hotel because I want to move out of my own life.

And my article still isn't done. Christ!

Rental Dog

I AM WALKING ON a nature trail in the morning, listening determinedly—as I have so many times in my life—to Joni Mitchell's *Blue*.

I crunch along the trail in some brand-new twenty-dollar Costco trek shoes I am happy with.

Coming toward me is a beaming, well-put-together fifty-ish or sixty-ish or seventy-ish (who knows?) woman, with a great sort of open Meredith Vieira face, completely hale and hearty, who is being pulled along by a gorgeous golden retriever. The two of them vibrate with health and goodness. They look so awesome I want to applaud. Her jogging suit looks organic and breathable, her sunglasses rock, his coat is shiny, his paws trot high, and he appears to be smiling.

I hear myself think: I want a dog! I want a dog just like that!

At which point I realize that, no, in fact I do not want a dog. I do not want a dog at all.

I think of the home-ware stores—Restoration Hardware, Crate and Barrel, Pottery Barn—which I continually wander through, both in person and in my mind. I always walk into a home-ware store and think, "Oh, what beautiful indigo Mexican hand-blown wineglasses." But then I will put them in our Energy Star dishwasher, which for some reason seems to be covering all of our glassware with a weird chalky coat, and then I will have to put them in the too-high cabinet where they don't quite fit.

Admiring the glassware, I think I am falling in love with a quartet of beautiful indigo Mexican hand-blown wineglasses, but I am really falling in love with a magical world where someone else always sets the table.

Which is to say I want that dog in that moment, yes.

I want a dog to pull me along the trail and to make me feel awesome.

But what I would want at the end of the trail is for a van full of twenty-something interns to pull up and take the dog from me. They can feed the dog and shop for kibble for it at Costco and give it the vaccinations it needs and they can go around their own homes sweeping the hair up. They can also go for the run I was supposed to have gone on, for that matter.

To the Bowl of Fruit meme and the Mexican Hand-Blown Wineglasses meme I suppose I can also add a Dog meme.

I suppose what that means is that I want a rental dog. I want to rent a dog to get only the good parts of a dog. To "essence" the dog.

When they train dogs to mix cocktails and deliver food, without me having to listen to mine natter on about its dog days, I will maybe entertain the thought then.

House Cat

THE GLOOMINGS ARE MORE frequent.

The darkies attack often.

The wraiths reach out.

That night in the hotel, a Westin, with blessedly crisp sheets, I lie awake at 3:24 A.M. as usual—melatonin, Tylenol PM, paired with a bottle of wine, and I can still drive an eighteen-wheeler. As I stare up into the darkness, all at once, the name Brian Hong surfaces in my consciousness, and I experience not a passing wave of despair, but despair simply moving in as a cold, straight tide.

I have no idea who Brian Hong is—I am filled with horror simply because of the name. Perhaps there is in fact a lone forgotten yellow Post-it, somewhere on my dining room table with its gas bills and Discover card solicitations and Blue Cross health-insurance forms, that reads "BRIAN HONG." Perhaps Brian Hong is the head of a small Asian nonprofit who several months ago earnestly if a bit keeningly e-mailed me, citing as a referral the name of a mutual friend, to ask if I would drive an hour down to San Pedro to give a free speech at a fund-raising benefit for a flailing youth center for depressed gay minority teens at 10:00 A.M. three months from now on a cloudy Wednesday.

On the one hand, as a longtime veteran of these sorts of appearances, I can no longer afford to humor the endless requests to do everything for free, particularly because no one treats you worse than the penniless. On the other hand, though, for me to categorically say no seems like a kick in the teeth to all the kids in the world who are already down; the result of this discomfiting indecision being that *I never replied to Brian Hong at all*, and so now, like that forgotten spongy corpse, he is coming after me in the middle of the night to gently (because that is Brian Hong's passive-aggressive way) but persistently (because that is also Brian Hong's passive-aggressive way) haunt me.

Or is Brian Hong a head person on one of my father's ghost checking accounts, an account I inadvertently share with him and then other dead Chinese relatives? And instead of coming after my father, who has cannily—as usual—left no trace or marker, is the ghost of Brian Hong coming from the far ends of the earth . . . for me?

AFTER TWO nights in a hotel, I know I should go home, but I just can't.

I have told Mr. Y to get out, and he has, moving his things to his coproducer Wilson's spacious Studio City abode, so it isn't a matter of needing a break from him, and from us.

It's just that the house is still there.

If only I could break up with my own house. I can't write there, think there, or focus there.

I feel I'm being strangled by it, by all these people's stuff—mine, Mr. Y's, and my children's. All the nests. I can no longer stand to be near any of it. It saps my chi. I don't want to be near any stuff I might remotely be considered to be responsible for. I don't want to be near that structure where everyone cants their chins up to the ceiling and says, "Where is—?" waiting for the food and the ketchup and the toilet paper to rain down magically. I don't want to be where socks go missing and smoke-alarm batteries need replacing and where my girls will say things to me like, "Mommy? According to this health unit we're studying, you need to buy pesticide-free vegetables," or "Mommy? I think you need to compost," to which I'm increasingly inclined to say: "Actually no, you have mistaken me for the sort of mommy who cares. Do it yourself. Or take your tiny almost-nonexistent college fund and hire someone to compost."

Thank God the girls are away for another ten days.

In my twenties and thirties I was into expansion.

Nearing fifty, I am now in retreat.

Full of loathing for this mortal coil, I just want to step outside the shell of myself, leave it behind like a wrinkled skin, and drift on, perhaps becoming a point somewhere beyond, hovering in space like an infinitesimal dust mote.

THE GOOD thing at midlife, though, is that if your friends have hung with you for as long as they have, they really do accept you. There really are fewer and fewer judgments. They are increasingly people to whom you can make the most awkward, rambling, inexact phone calls.

To wit: "Uh, hi, Judith? Where did you tell me you just bought your new house? Was it off Coldwater somewhere? I'd love to come see it sometime to get some . . . er . . . remodeling tips. Would it be convenient to come around in, say, oh, I don't know . . . one hour?"

And here comes Vague Gambit Two: "I'm going to be in your part of the Valley anyway. I've been thinking of maybe renting an office there, as when I do my girls' school drop-offs and pickups I have all this time to kill in the middle of the day." This is technically true: I have been thinking about getting an office in the Valley, but for what I can afford it would be a shoebox, and then I would have to haul in some furniture and a coffeemaker and it's like starting all over again at the Pirate's Cove and I'm already tired.

What I would prefer is to wash up on the porch of one of my girlfriends with a lovely well-kept home in the middle of the day with my computer and my work satchel, as though her house were some kind of benevolent public library. If peckish I would like to do a little light refrigerator raiding. If thirsty I would like to pour myself Pellegrino that I myself have not hauled in in a case from Costco. I would like to be a houseguest in my own sunny cottage who works during the day and then appears at 5:00 P.M. for cocktail hour and light chatter before we all sit down for a robust evening meal, cooked by Hannah Gruen (the motherly housekeeper in the Nancy Drew books) or similar. Or I could even curl up in a basket at the foot of somebody's bed. I could be someone's cat.

Amazingly Judith returns my call immediately—she happens to be in, and would love to show me her house.

JUDITH LIVES on—can you believe it?—Sunswept Drive. These are the street names found only in fiction! And in Los Angeles.

It is impossible to find—nested in a zillion twists and turns. This makes me love it even more. It is a place to truly get lost.

"Welcome!" Judith says, arms out, in a muslin shift and ballet slippers, gliding up the drive. "Welcome!" Oh the lightness of step of the child-free!

What ensues is a short whirlwind tour of her pretty amazing property—it's nested on a hillside with multiple angled levels and skylights. Above the glittering pool is a vast and gleaming open floor plan. It's something you could practically roller-skate through and then arrive, skidding slightly, at the perfect lipstick-red art nouveau divan . . .

But most amazingly of all, there is no clutter. Books are so perfectly arranged in custom-built walls of bookshelves that they actually look like art.

"Roland did it—isn't it wonderful?" she says.

"I can't even imagine how he did that," I say.

Judith and Roland are an interesting couple. Judith is a screenwriter, Roland is a sculptor. He is Swiss, and he has a discreet, comfortable amount of family money. While they've been together for more than ten years, they have never married. And I must say, curiously, I find the most remarkable facet of their cliffside home is that Judith and Roland have separate entrances. Up above is her work space, a sunny if fairly tiny aerie; below is his rambling bachelor office and studio, overlooking the pool. ("I don't swim," she says. "I hate water.") In the middle level are the vast open living room and dining room and giant kitchen.

"It's his kitchen," she says wryly. "He designed it. As you can see, it's a very manly kitchen. It's where he plays. They say the kitchen is the new garage." It is indeed a very masculine kitchen, all dark cabinets and stone counters and ordered rows of gleaming restaurant-quality appliances and stainless-steel kitchen tools, as clean a space as one would imagine one might need to perform surgery.

"He's the performance cook," she laughs. "You should see what he's making tonight. Oh!" She turns to me eagerly. "Oh! Are you around? Maybe you should come for dinner!"

My evil plan is working. I haven't been planning on ever leaving. It is all I can do not to handcuff myself to a whisper-shut drawer.

I am now staring at a brand-new retaining wall they have built, to create a multidecked Zen front garden. It is the sort of project I would never be able to figure out spatially or pull the trigger on. Mr. X was always the one getting quotes and getting things fixed and cursing because all-new copper piping would cost four thousand dollars, but he would always go ahead anyway, and as a result his homes (two bungalows next door to

each other) all look very well maintained. In his absence, I now
see the huge gaping life hole that he has left.

Mr. X kept me together. Now I am in collapse. Because I
thought what I needed in a man was to stand and gossip in my
kitchen.

I think back to that ur-anecdote I tell myself about Mr. X
setting down his suitcases and saying, "The roof needs fixing."
Now, without him, I realize . . . the fact of the matter is that
my roof is still unfixed.

It was Mr. X who took care of all of these matters, invisi-
bly, like an angel Gabriel in the house. I miss him deeply like
a phantom limb. He had roots in the earth, and his steady
internal clock brought a calm and security that I never even
noticed.

Oh God.

I miss Mr. X.

Never mind all the loneliness and separate TV shows we
liked and the kids and twenty years of life rolling by.

He was my rock. And actually still is. Father of my children. Salt of the earth.

I ask how Judith has managed to figure out all the projects
she is showing me—the retaining wall and the foundation and
the fencing and the refurbished pool deck.

Hand on her chest, she leans forward and says, as lovingly
as Tony says "Maria" in *West Side Story*: "Luis."

There is a knock at the door.

"Oh, there he is!" she exclaims, almost too trillingly.

Luis is a perhaps-forty-five-year-old Guatemalan handyman clutching several bags from Home Depot. "Hello, Mrs. Judith! You want I put motion detectors in today?"

"Yes! And would you like some coffee?"

"Yes I would!"

"I always make him coffee," Judith purrs to me.

Luis, apparently, is the secret ingredient that makes their domestic life hum. Sure! I think. Who *couldn't* make that work? Lovely home, big pot of Swiss family money, and staff! But Judith is also a very calm domestic organizer. Judith gives Luis a constant running list of repairs, and he is there every day. This particular thing she does is a very Old World skill.

Judith invites me to hang out in what they call the library, a perfect little tree house hovering above the foliage. I congratulate myself on the perfect casting of my perfect friend and her perfect house. There is actually a pristine guest bathroom attached—it has lavender-slate-colored tile, a bathtub under a glass-cubed window, and I see that extra touch: She has even lit an aromatherapy candle for me. And in the windowsill in an alcove beyond? A perfect blue bowl of fruit. Meyer lemons. I have found it—the meme of the perfect bowl of fruit.

I open my laptop and words pour forth. All around is the distant hum of a home and puttering and distant conversation and also, always, the sound of Luis's distant hammering. It is soothing, and one feels not cramped but gently enveloped as though with a soft pashmina shawl. The AC breathes steadily, like a spray, and outside is a tinkling fountain.

And now here is this marvelous thing that happens at a quarter to twelve. Judith slides open the doors, sticks her cropped blond head in, and says, "Lunch is tuna salad on English muffin. Okay? It's what I tend to have. Don't worry—it's small."

And a moment later Jude slides open the doors, glides down the stairs in her ballet slippers, and slips a plate next to me with a cloth napkin. It is an English muffin with tuna salad and scallions and dill and, "Oh my God—is this ginger?" I ask. "It's delicious!"

Her statement, delivered with a toss of the head: "I was single for a long time, I never had children, I've never had to be reasonable."

WHAT HAVE I been searching for? What have I been yearning for? In the serenity of Sunswept Drive, I suddenly know, my mind calmed and soothed by the quiet, sure ticking of a well-run house. Day by day in my frenetic, chaotic home, why am I so unglued by the leaking Ziploc bag or the microwave-deformed Gladware that now doesn't quite close? I realize now that what I am seeing in all these small secret totems is evidence that no one is taking care of me! No one! *No one!* And that is no small thing.

Instead of a man, perhaps what I need at this point is a spa, or staff, or a hotel. Even though I'm not doing a show right now, I wish I were still being treated like a diva. That is not a terribly attractive thought but in the moment it feels true.

The sun sets over the Valley; six women, friends and dinner guests of Judith's, sit on the terrace; just beyond, Roland, in his scraggly, scraped-back white ponytail and coveralls, is busy grilling at some giant metal contraption that looks like a small wind tunnel; he is flanked by two equally boyish, middle-aged guy friends who, like him, look a little high and a little surprised about being high, and who are holding beers. Brazilian Suba music is playing; wineglasses clink; there's muted laughter. The oversize wooden smorgas-table to our right groans with good wine and European waters and exotic aperitifs and mini-bouquets of artisanal olives and a rustic cheese board flanked by a rustic pâté board. And of course one must have fresh-baked bread, sourdough baguettes and herb-seeded boules and whole-grain *filones*.

What with the tiki lamps descending like modern dancers in a snakelike line down the hill, these are sights, sounds, and cadences that remind me a bit of my twenty-something years in Los Angeles. The difference, of course, is that we creative-class folk are now all forty-something and fifty-something and sixty-something and the air is refreshingly free of sexual tension. No one gives a fuck about the big proscenium drama of heterosexuality anymore, no one believes that escape from life's basic tedium will come in the corpus of another person. Staring unapologetically into the grill are the men of manopause, and clinking pinot grigio in a circle are the women of menopause: the undatables.

There is Wendy, a radio-producer friend of mine who was tormented, through most of her forties, by a passionate yet thoroughly miserable affair she was having with a married colleague who, in the end, never mind all his protestations to the contrary, never did leave his family. Rounding the horn of fifty, though, in the next turn, her life canoe suddenly shot forward into the calm happy waters of home. This came via a depressed real estate market, with unheard-of bargains everywhere.

"After all those years with Jonathan," she says, "I could finally dream in a new way. You know that house hunting has its own kind of romance. The stately Victorian, the charming Craftsman, or even the 'rambling midcentury stunner with great bones.'" Of course her budget could only sustain an eight-hundred-square-foot cottage in Highland Park, but . . . "Unlike Jonathan," she continues, "my little house is fixable. It's something I can work on. It can be constantly improved. I can put effort in and get results out. If I'd just been able to buy a house before I met Jonathan, I would have saved myself a lot of trauma."

Petra, a marketing executive, has been trying to date again now that her divorce is eight years old and her kids are long up and gone. But she's losing the strength for it. A toothsomely attractive blonde (she is fifty-five but looks thirty-five, with Kelly Ripa sinews), she keeps getting set up with eligible men on the Westside, but due to her workout regime and desire to stay slim, Petra finds she cannot really "look forward to" dinner at 7:00 P.M.

"I guess we should go hiking instead or something, but that's not really a date."

She had a recent taxing outing with a Cedars-Sinai anesthesiologist. They could barely stretch the date to two hours. He was, quite frankly, "a little stiff."

"Of *course* he's a little stiff!" We all laugh, easing into the growing comfortable darkness. "He's an anesthesiologist!"

As we undatable women natter away, though, with our garden-variety shots about men, I realize the balance of this particular festive hill is dependent on the three men down below, wordlessly grilling. It is as though the men are deep in the earth, in some sort of Lord of the Rings–type way, shoveling coals. In so doing, in holding down that ballast, they are keeping some part of this mysterious clockwork going. They blessedly do not react to our critiques or parse our language; they sip beers, they turn coals, they keep going.

I suddenly wonder, thinking back to my own domestic situation, if my trivial yet painful domestic conflicts with Mr. Y have something to do with how my generation of women first encountered men. Our first experience living with them was not as blushing newlyweds but rather in street-battling our sweatpants-wearing, *Tron*-watching brethren in co-ed dorms in college (the spattering lentil soup, dish-filled sinks, baskets of moldy laundry). Perhaps it is because of that that it sometimes it feels as if we are having the same peevish brother-sister fight over and over again, even though it's thirty years later, everyone's fifty, and the dorm is our house. Even today it seems in some ways I still haven't mentally graduated from college. If I have twenty boxes of books to move from the basement, in a reflex, I immediately think, What guy friends should I call to help me? I think this even though half my fifty-something guy friends have a torn rotator cuff and would not even help me if they could, nor am I a cute college girl whom they have boffed or might like to boff or whom anyone will ever boff or who would even look good on Saturday-moving day in Daisy Mae shorts. I am a haggard, ill-tempered almost-fifty-year-old woman with her own money who needs to drive her ass down to U-Haul, pick up two Mexicans, pay them twenty bucks each, and be done in an hour.

I think, too, as I look toward the trio of men around the flame, about the husbands, boyfriends, and friends whose company I have so deeply enjoyed over the years. Necking, dancing, sitting on a stoop with a beer, playing pool . . . Men can be such pleasurable companions. Instead of shrei-ing at them for chore work or fixing faucets or paying the property tax, perhaps they are more like these exotic artisanal beings we need to place carefully in tissue paper to preserve their wonderful tobacco and cardamom flavor notes. As far as a warm body in bed, men are nicer to talk to than dogs, and if their domestic skills stink, ours are worse.

As Roland grills and bastes and sautés, and as he continues to put out headily aromatic platters of meat for the group (lamb, sausage, pork, beef tenderloin), with aioli and *chimichurri* sauce, our female conversation, like bubbling *prosecco*, spills forward.

"Well," I say, "here's what I think. I think part of the problem with modern heterosexual relationships is that all women secretly yearn for in the world is not one husband, but four. What do you think?"

Everyone agrees and jumps into the game. We tease it out and come up with, essentially: "The Four Husbands of the Apocalypse."

I lay the initial groundwork by suggesting that the first two husbands are, as I've lived it myself, Mr. X and Mr. Y.

"Which is to say your first husband—Mr. X—is your financial partner. He's not necessarily the financial provider, because so many of us women make money. But I think of the first husband as that calm, intelligent partner with whom to negotiate the tedious financial technicalities of life—the 401Ks, college funds, Metropolitan Life health-insurance plans. The second husband—Mr. Y—is the feelings guy who actually talks to you."

"Oh God," Wendy says. "The feelings guy. Mr. Y. That was totally Jonathan." Her married man. "He was all about the glass of chardonnay proffered with soulful active listening at the end of the day before the roaring fire. Before going home late to his wife."

"I think the second husband provides pampering—" Petra adds.

"What sort of pampering?" I want to know. "Do you mean like massage?"

"Oh no!" she says. "No massage. Which some 'date nights' are supposed to feature. Yuck."

Everyone immediately agrees that no sensible human wouldn't prefer a massage from a professional, because when your "mate" rubs your back, instead of relaxation there is the tension of anticipating what reciprocation will be required—five minutes of sex, or worse, a twenty-minute massage back.

"I feel that second husband is a complex role. While it falls to the second husband to provide amorous relations if needed, for some women it would be enough or even preferred for Mr. Y to function as the gentlemanly squire. That's what *I* thought it was, anyway. Maurice Tempelsman holding the umbrella in the rain. Or I suppose he could even be gay—David Gest to Liza Minnelli—'Madame will be home at seven, ready the Vosges chocolates, draw her a bath!'—although, of course, that ended after sixteen months in lawsuits, beatings, herpes, etc."

"Doesn't Sir Elton John have a Mr. Y?" Judith asks.

"Probably."

We decide that third husband—Mr. Z—is Mr. Fixit. "The burly stevedore, cowboy, Brawny Paper Towel man," says Judith.

Wendy agrees: "Mr. Fixit wheels out the garbage cans, repairs the electronic garage door opener, and resets the computerized tankless water heater." She sighs. "When smoke alarms suddenly scream off at 3:00 A.M. due to low batteries—which it seems is all they do—it is Mr. Z who leaps out of bed with hernia-threatening vigor to still them, with the giant thick baseball bat he of course keeps at the side of the bed."

"Luis can do that," Judith points out. "Maybe you just need a really good handyman. I'll give you his number."

"Fourth husband—Mr. Q—is, I think, the cheerful intern," I conclude. "Mr. Q executes whatever tiny necessary tasks you request without argument. He accepts a stack of envelopes and addresses them, picks up the dry cleaning before noon if needed, is on call for 24/7 emergency kid transport, and, best of all, when handed a grocery list he will return with—get this—that grocery list's exact items."

"But the problem is, no one man can possibly be all these four people!" Judith exclaims. "Mr. Xs are notoriously bad at processing feelings, Mr. Ys are notoriously bad at fixing things, macho Mr. Zs hate to be micromanaged, and Mr. Qs do not actually exist in real life, although in modern marriages husbands and wives often *do* treat each other as interns: 'You pick up the dry cleaning!' 'No *you* should, by five! And put it on the United Miles card, not Bank of America!' "

"Well, like I said, I guess I'm grateful to have had Mr. X and Mr. Y in sequence," I say. "The way I think of it: Mr. X did my twenty-something unemployment, thirty-something career angst, the death of my mother, two pregnancies, and also that whole forty-something mess of breast-feeding, insomnia, and public-school panic . . . followed by the traumatic affair and a swift divorce. Mr. Y was going to be handling menopause . . . or, as I've figured it out so far, in the twenty-first century, your first husband is the provider; your second husband is the one who talks to you; my third husband will be a cat. If I am lucky."

"But see how you're thinking of the men as servicing you," Roland says, as he lays down another large platter, which looks like a choucroute. "You're not thinking of men as individual people. And for their part, I think many men would also like not one wife but four."

"Oh sure," says Petra. "Wife number one—Rebecca, the endlessly hectoring if laudably responsible mother of their children. It is she who drives the school admissions applications, doctors' appointments, allergy lists."

"Wife number two," Wendy pipes up. "Doubles tennis partner Cheryl, the smart sassy business wife who trills: 'Last-minute dinner with your Intel colleagues at seven? What fortuitous timing, when the NASDAQ is at 4650! What fun—I'll show up in either the black cocktail dress or the red—I'll surprise you!' "

"Yes, just like that tennis-playing gal in *Carnal Knowledge*," says Petra.

"I love that movie!" says Judith.

"You guys are nuts," says Roland's friend Tom. "It shows how little you know about men. Wife number two is only about one thing: She loves and follows your favorite sports team."

"Well, I bet I can guess wife number three," Wendy presses on. "Wife number three—the sex-obsessed nympho who herself has seven roles: St. Pauli girl, French maid, Catholic schoolgirl . . ."

"Dallas Cowboys cheerleader," Petra adds.

"Well, I'll give you that one," Tom says. The men murmur their assent.

"And for wife number four," I say, "Giordana, the curvaceous Italian earth-mother pasta-at-midnight wife who is always saying: 'Come on over, late, anytime! I've made all this pasta!' Right?"

Everyone stares at me in nonrecognition.

"I think that's your own fantasy," Judith says. "Men eat pasta all the time. They don't care."

"I guess I'm just oddly jonesing for that Giada gal on the Food Network," I say.

It is now that Roland's friend Craig, a journalist, who has until now been but orange ash glowing in a gray cloud of smoke in the darkness, gives his two cents' worth.

"Sure," he says aggressively, flicking down his cigarette butt. "I could pick apart my marriage. I could even do it in public like half my female colleagues do—like you, Sandra—you women who make your living at it. But if male authors wrote half the things about their wives that female authors wrote about their husbands, we'd be run out of town! There was some Sunday magazine piece recently where the writer—good Lord!—she went on for page after page complaining about her husband's cooking! He's a great cook, sure, makes great meals, and watches the kids, and rolls out the trash cans but she feels—boo-hoo!—that he lingers too long in the kitchen and buys too many expensive ingredients!"

He leans in with half a sneer: "Meanwhile, a wife can gain thirty pounds during pregnancy, keep it on for decades, and God forbid the husband ever utters a peep about it. A peep!"

Everyone halts for a moment.

Craig makes a good point.

And of course he is right about that.

He abruptly excuses himself for the evening to go home. Craig is still married.

DESSERT IS petits fours and other floating-cloud, ornate-flower-invention desserts from Judith and Roland's favorite Studio City bakery. Everyone applauds our cook, and Judith alights on Roland's now-collapsed lap, in her pale evening gauze and her ballet slippers, to deliver a pronouncement.

"I was married once," she says, "years before I met Roland. My ex—who was an academic—and I used to argue about the best way to broil a salmon. Neither of us was grateful for the gift that someone else might cook it, albeit slightly incorrectly. It was a horrible way to live.

"In the end, I think, if you're going to live with someone, there should be rules. Each person must have their own bathroom, absolutely. Roland and I even have our own bedrooms, which is wonderful because he snores."

"As does she," Roland adds.

Judith lifts her hands. "How would I know?"

"Indeed."

"I think in the end, however, when you find ways to be together, there is the matter of coffee. Which is to say, imagine someone you supposedly love brings you a cup of coffee. Perhaps that cup of coffee is too strong, too weak, too milky, too sugary, not enough of all of the above, whatever. I would say instead of critiquing all the parts of the coffee that aren't right, just say thank you. Just appreciate the gift of coffee. Even if you have to dump it into the sink when they're not looking. Say thank you.

"Staff helps, too," Judith adds, as Roland takes her hand and both get up.

"Also dancing," Roland says, pulling her in, as they move together to some bossa nova.

"See?" Judith says. "Who cares if he snores? He's a great dancer."

With a surge of fondness, under the glowing night sky, I think of Mr. Y, who is also a great dancer, the best. I think of texting him some fond short message, to get that little hit of him.

But I know all too well this is the top of the cycle, and tomorrow—with all of its customary realities and harrowing exigencies—will be the bottom. To contact Mr. Y would be like continuing to punish him, continuing to whip him around in this laundry cycle.

What is the point of calling Mr. Y? We've both done this already.

And actually, it's the end of our romance.

I fell in love with Mr. Y at Burning Man based on such a hopelessly absurd romantic notion. This notion did not occur to me in the moment when I told him I guessed I loved him. Rather, it came to me in the moment when he had—surprisingly—admitted that he always figured we'd end up together when we were older. He may have just meant it with a shrug. He wasn't planning to do anything about it. Perhaps he was a bit lazy. But I had woven it into such a high romantic Merchant-Ivory notion. The notion was that, like some Good Soldier, he was content to patiently bide his time for three decades, and in the meantime was content to dedicate himself, without reward, to chivalrously serving me.

What a foolish idea!

When I now picture Mr. Y's face, all hard-eyed and contorted, while he flies at me in rage ("You need help wiping your own ass!"), I realize that we had had mismatching expectations. He now has only revulsion for me because I have been under a diva illusion. And as for me, the tide has washed out and I am no longer in love with this person, because all along I had thought he was different from other men.

How so? This was a straight man you could converse with for ten hours about movies, food, friends, family, romances we had in our twenties, scuzzy college dorms we had lived in, gardening (how we both wanted to but didn't), dogs (how we liked them but balked at caring for them), spicy versus sweet mustard, methods of dry cleaning, sex, religion, and our feelings, and never run out of things to talk about. This was a man you could call day or night who would always pick up. This was a man happy—even delighted—to take you dress shopping, with far more patience than I myself might have for this process. (I am the sort of person who will run out of Ross Dress for Less screaming, whereas he is very interested in comparing sale-priced belts.) This was a man who had known me (or at least parts of me) for ten years, and who slid easily and organically into the highest flights of poetry and romance, who needed no seducing. This was a man with whom I didn't have to pretend to be someone else or hide different parts of myself in order to earn his love. I had thought he was the sunny island my shipwreck had landed on. I had thought he was the final safe harbor. I had thought he was this calm glowing orb hovering in a cloudless blue sky of unconditional love. I suppose I thought he was my mother, or at least the manifestation of the love of my mother, or perhaps her living ghost.

As I say, as though watching a movie, "How sad."

The Sudden Death of My Father

MY FATHER CALLS ME in terror. He can't get out of bed. It is Sunday. Thomas has weekends off. This is typically fine but . . .

"Help me," he whispers.

I feel a panic flood of cortisol.

It is not like my dad has been in exactly perfect health over the last decade.

After age seventy-eight, if you asked my father, "How are you?" he would already exclaim: "I'm dying!" At his eightieth birthday party, when he tremulously lifted his centimeter of red wine while watching my girlfriends dance, I mourned his visible frailty. At eighty-two, he was passing out on bus benches, hitting his head, causing his doctors to insist on a pacemaker (which he refused). By eighty-five, battling Parkinson's, he was still hobbling down to the beach to attempt rickety calisthenics and swimming, but "he's barely swimming in those two feet of water," Kaitlin worried. "It's more like falling."

By eighty-seven, he was physically slowing, like a clock

winding down, and then he started, under great protest, to use a wheelchair on and off, but then . . . he seemed to plateau. Indeed, recently, with Thomas's extraordinary care, because he was lifted everywhere, and spoon-fed, he actually seemed to be coming back.

When I brought the girls to visit most recently, he was sleeping in his daybed with a pair of socks over his eyes. From under the socks, he said to Hannah, "Oh, you're pretty. Are you one of the mean girls in your school?" and for some reason she immediately fell over laughing. She got his strange Martian brand of humor. I have no reason why.

My irascible dad's will to live—to watch PBS, to eat ice cream, to shuffle through the garden on a walker—is strong. You can hear it in his voice.

But not today.

This is a different, hollowed-out-sounding man. A ghost already gone.

A pulse-pounding ninety-minute drive through traffic later, I storm into the house and rush to his bed, which happens for reasons of maximizing rental space, to be in the dining room. I find to my panic—"Papa? Papa?"—that I cannot rouse him. He lies in that waxy, inert, folded-up pose that looks unmistakably like death (I had seen it when my mother died of early Alzheimer's at sixty-nine).

I dial Kaitlin in San Francisco. We haven't talked in ages, but now the Margaret Thatcher silence must be broken.

"This is it—it's really it—Papa's dead," I sob over the phone.

"Oh no," she breathes softly, like a mourning dove.

We both exhale.

And yet, as the dust motes dance in the familiar golden light of our family home, my sister and I find ourselves spontaneously, tumblingly, observing to each other how we are sad . . . and yet oddly at peace.

Yes, our history with this man has been beyond checkered: In our childhood he had been cruelly cheap (no Scholastic Book Fair, no heat, no Christmas); in our teens he had been unforgivably mean to my mother (they had those horrible fights about money, he cursed at her, called her bad words in front of us); in my twenties, I myself rebelled (by dropping out of science!) and fled; in my thirties I softened and we became wry friends—why not, he couldn't harm me now; in my forties, sensing that these were the last days of a fading elder, the memories of whom I would reflect on with increasing nostalgia, the door opened for real affection, even a kind of gratitude. After all, I had benefited professionally from using him as fodder for my writing, as he had benefited financially for years by forging my signature on all those ghost checking accounts—the great circle of life.

The point is, no matter how vexing and impossible and just plain *unfatherly* your father is, you only have one. When he goes, something is gone that you are never going to get back. One of those things, of course, is your childhood, or the possibility of reviving the illusion of ever having had a happy one . . . which was long gone anyway. And, in the end, my father does have a certain authenticity and trueness. He is always uniquely himself. And when I lie on my own deathbed, that is one thing in life that I will miss. Or if I don't truly miss it, it will at least give me a great cosmic chuckle.

Which is to say, standing on this silvery-lighted sandbar of midlife, somewhat complexly, there is real grief now at seeing my father go. Then again, I am a big girl—actually, a middle-aged woman, with some one thousand hours of therapy behind me—and, chin up, I will get through it. Unlike in the case of our mother, who had left too abruptly and too early, my business here is done. It's a time of endings, it appears. But it's all right. Life is actually so long that I have successfully completed my Kübler-Ross stages.

So perhaps the timing of my father's passing, though sad, is fortuitous.

The conundrum this morning in the dining room, however, is that although my father isn't rousable, I can't say for sure that he is actually dead. (Remember that he has that lizardlike resting pulse of 34, so even in his waking state he's sort of like the undead.) He doesn't seem to be conspicuously breathing, but neither is he conspicuously hardening.

I pose this conundrum to Kaitlin who has, among other things, a master's degree in biology. Tormented pause. She suggests I call the Malibu paramedics and have them make the official call.

I do so, awkwardly explaining to 911 that while my father is not quite alive, he is also not thoroughly dead. He doesn't seem to be suffering or struggling to breathe or hemorrhaging blood or anything. He's just sort of a lukewarm log. Whatever is happening is not acute.

Within five minutes a massive fire truck roars up and half a dozen buff Malibu EMTs pile out, like the cast of some hit CBS prime-time drama. They strap my eighty-nine-year-old father onto a gurney, stick an IV in, zip him off, sirens blazing, to the emergency room, and immediately start mobile triage work on all of his vitals.

An hour later, a surprisingly benign diagnosis? Simple dehydration. (He wasn't drinking the water that Thomas is always exhorting him to—only coffee and orange juice.)

In short, with a sudden angry snort, my father wakes up!

"Son of a bitch!" he yells at me. "Why did you bring me here?" He immediately demands ice cream.

Jesus!

What am I supposed to do?

Where is this all going?

The Caregiver's Journey

I RECEIVE A GIFT and a note from my friend Patty. The note reads: "I am thinking of you during these difficult times with your father. I know when caring for my own mother, it was both the hardest and most beautiful experience I have ever had. What really helped me was this Adult Daughters retreat in Esalen (brochure enclosed)."

The gift is a pashmina, lavender-infused mini-chocolates, and a calendar featuring flowers and inspirational proverbs and sayings about something horrible (featuring a nautilus shell) called the Caregiver's Journey. The note continues, "I love this quote from Gail Sheehy from her book *Passages in Caregiving*: 'It opens up the greatest possibilities for true intimacy and reconnection at the deepest level. The sharing of strengths and vulnerabilities, without shame, fosters love. And for some caregivers, this role offers a chance in Second Adulthood to compose a more tender sequel to the troubled family drama of our First Adulthood. We can become better than our younger selves.'"

Really? I mean, *really*?

Gail Sheehy and *Passages*—what a laugh! She will live to rewrite *Passages* for another fifty years. To humor the occasion, I open the book at random and read this:

> In my books and speeches since 1995, when I published *New Passages*, I keep predicting liberation ahead—the advent of a Second Adulthood, starting in one's midforties and fifties. At that proud age, having checked off most 'shoulds,' people generally feel a new sense of mastery. Haven't you done your best to please your parents, your mentor, your boss, and your mate, and now it's time for you? The children are making test flights on their way to piloting solo. Your parents have become giddy globe-trotters, piling up frequent-flier miles and e-mailing playful photos of themselves riding camels. . . . Now you can finally earn that degree, start your own business, run for office, master another language, invent something, or write that book you keep mulling.

I have an urge to find Patty and throw the book in her face. But I don't.

I carefully place the Caregiver's Journey calendar in the recycling bin, and immediately wolf all the chocolates.

Ladies of the Lake

MR. Y HAS LEFT a cryptic message. Still living at Wilson's sprawling bachelor pad, presumably, he and I have not seen each other in four weeks, and have only exchanged a few texts. His first-ever phone message is friendly and guarded and wry, in that sort of punch-one-in-the-arm-type way, inviting me to be his date to the closing-night party of *Jam City*. It sounds awful. I am telling Kaitlin about this as we round Balboa Lake (yes, we do have the occasional lake in Los Angeles) on one of those healthful walks she enjoys. It's so windy we are less walking than beavering our way, heads down with determination, around the lake. All around us other ladies in Asics and visors are also beavering around the lake. It's almost as though we women power the lake, as though we're its worried turbine engine.

"How is it going otherwise?" she asks me.

"Oh, it's tough," I say. "Grimly I clock forward. Everything is emotionally flat. There's nothing in life to look forward to. Every day I Scotch-tape myself together, I staple myself together, I glue myself together, and get up to forge forward into, well, this wind. I do it for the girls. I stay in there. I sledgehammer into the ice, put my ice pick in, grimly hang on to the side of the mountain.

"I found myself thinking, you know, of Mrs. Sedaris as she appeared in David Sedaris's story 'Let It Snow.' I taught that in my writing class last year. There were too many snow days in a row so, going crazy from their constant company, Mrs. Sedaris locked the children out of the house, and sat at the kitchen table quietly smoking and drinking. Then she fell down in the snow and lost her shoe. The children collected her."

"And?"

"And I realize I am at the point in my life where, instead of thinking of myself as one of the bright semi-young lights of *This American Life* as at one distant time I used to be, I actually think a lot about Mrs. Sedaris. I am not David or Amy Sedaris, I am really much closer to their mother, who sits at the kitchen table during the day haplessly smoking and drinking and who loses her shoe in the snow. Oh God."

"Hmm," she says. "What else are you reading?"

"Good question. It's hard to find a book to get into these days. Since Mr. Y's been gone, I just want something comforting at night, like a cozy English country cottage of a book. In the middle of a sunny meadow where the bees *bzz-bzz-bzz* and the dragonflies go *zzp-zzp-zzp*. I want a book to gently entertain and lift and then tranquilize me. I want kind of a Zoloft of a book."

"I never travel without a P. G. Wodehouse or a David

Lodge. I just adore those books. I bring my foldable night-light along, and everything's perfect."

"Well, I always think that sort of comforting midafternoon voice is going to come from Anna Quindlen, your funny, smart, sensible friend who sort of always has your back. So when I was staying at Judith's, I took to my temple-like guest bath Anna Quindlen's *Lots of Candles, Plenty of Cake*, a book I thought should be its own cozy warm bath.

"But while reading it I soon began to freak out and feel like a failure. I realized that Anna Quindlen is a warm, sensible, self-deprecating essayist who also happens to still be happily married (no blow ups, no affairs) to her high-school sweetheart after decades and decades and who very sensibly gave up drinking, flat, in her twenties because she thought it wasn't a terribly wise idea. Her worry is that she has collected a few too many plush throw pillows in her beautiful home with her husband whom she loves.

"God, I felt like a hideous monster failure with a crippled fucking claw. Anna Quindlen was a judgmental beeyotch masquerading as a nice person, and I hate her. I realize this puts me in the can't-win position of attacking a clearly very nice and successful person, with my crippled fucking metaphorical claw. But if only we could see women crash around a bit more, particularly in middle age. If only our cropped Katie Couric hair could be let messily down.

"I mean," I press on, "I think of a famous poet I know whom we'll just called Devorah. Devorah was interviewing for a good university job teaching poetry. She is both celebrated and a bit scary—with a dessicated overthin look that would look amazing on any of the Rolling Stones but that people might perhaps find off-putting on a fifty-six-year-old woman. Even though she is incredibly thin and wears cool rock-and-roll belts.

"Anyhoo, when she was invited to sit down for the interview she declined, saying, 'It's just that last night I had so much sex my pussy is sore!' It so very much cheers me when a sister lowers the bar. Thank you, Devorah. Okay, K. Your turn. What have you been reading?"

"Oh my gosh, in my book group we've been reading the best book—*Oops, I Married My Mother!*"

"Oh boy!"

"Sure! Well, it's not really the best book, it's a little on the nose, and she seems to have borrowed all her concepts from other writers. But it was handy to have all these ideas in one slim manual. Okay, so she posits this not-terribly-new theory that whatever wounds we suffered in childhood, via the dynamics of our parents, we carry forward into our adult relationships. Sometimes what we do in fact is marry our mothers, as I did with my ex-husband, Gerald."

"Sure," I say glumly. "That's nothing new."

"With Gerald, I was always patrolling the perimeter, trying to make sure everything was okay in just the same way I used to hover nervously over Mama. Then he got depressed and let everything go to seed, and I probably enabled him as I just kept caretaking him and caretaking him until I realized I no longer wanted to be married to a depressed, fat, unemployed alcoholic. But now of course with my second husband, Steven, I have a totally different relationship. If anything, he's sometimes a bit too independent. So now I get to be the whiny one.

"But you know what, Mouseling," she says turning to me and calling me by my childhood name. "You talk a lot about being lonely when Mr. Y is gone. Lonely. This is even though you guys generally spend more time together than humanly possible—you used to go together to the gym, for crying out loud! And you were never 'lonely' with Mr. X. Aside from that one time early on with Mr. X, when he was in Spain for two weeks and you couldn't take it and were crying on the phone and then he sent you that plane ticket—"

"He did?" What's curious is I don't even remember the incident. It's hard to remember crying on the phone with Mr. X, but now I vaguely recall that that must have been true.

"Uh-huh. Oh yeah. And when you were a little girl and we had twin beds, you used to flop out your leg to cross the bridge so your leg would actually be in my bed. Also at night we used to sometimes pile into Mama's bed, and she would get so crowded and fed up she'd go back into one of our empty beds."

"Well, that part I remember," I say.

"The thing is, I know you. And you are not by nature a lonely person. You are by nature interested and focused and busy doing ten things at a time that you enjoy."

"Uh-huh."

"Mr. Y has put up with a ton from you, for so many years you don't even see it. The man loves you so much—he destroyed his life for you. But just like I'm always patrolling the perimeter to make sure everyone around me is happy, which is my pathology, it's like you're also patrolling the perimeter, always alert, on watch, to make sure that love is not going away. It's like you're asking him to prove it over and over again: Don't take that job.

Come home on time. Don't be late. Call me back quickly. And he always does, pretty much, but it's never enough."

"It does feel like that," I admit.

"But maybe you're going to have to let that go. Look. You lost your mother quite young to Alzheimer's disease, and that's sad. That's really sad. Starting from nineteen you didn't really have a mother, and she had been everything to you. But you can sit with those feelings and let them move through you. It's okay. You don't have a mother and that is sad. The author of *Oops* says we don't sit enough with our grief and let our bodies process it. It's grief we've sometimes been holding on to for decades. And that's okay until the age of fifty. After fifty our bodies can't hold it anymore without inflicting self-damage. So our health will begin to suffer with the burden of carrying all this stuff around.

"Apparently when you actually let yourself feel an emotion— rather than pushing it off because you think it will swallow you—well—when you actually let yourself feel it, and sit with it, it goes away. Maybe it's okay to want to be loved, and just the fact that your mom died does not make you unlovable. Maybe it will all end up okay. Maybe you can have a joyful life. Maybe you can become the man you always wanted to marry."

Kaitlin makes me write a letter, and here it is:

Dear Mr. Y,

Here is my letter of apology. You have been a good and loyal person who has gone beyond the call of duty for too many years. I never realized how much you generously gave, I took it for granted, and I humbly thank you for all the help you have con-

tributed that has helped me prosper, both creatively and financially and as a person.

I am sorry in the course of our relationship I have behaved so monstrously, which has helped to destroy this magical feeling we once had. At its best, my time with you was truly the most fun I've ever had.

I think I have some unresolved issues that have to do with missing my mom and feeling untethered with my dad and honestly really wanting be taken care of, occasionally, by someone.

Perhaps that's the wrong role to try to plug a man into at this point in my life. Our relationship began with you in a kind of caretaker role, and I naively misread everything. Nobody's fault but mine.

I wish you well in all your future endeavors and sincerely hope you find happiness.

The greatest thing I can hope to achieve is, if in five years' time, I can say truthfully that I am your friend. If not your huckleberry friend, then just a good friend.

Love,
Me

The Great Retreat

REGRETTABLY, MY SOJOURN AT Sunswept is over.
I am back in my house. I am back with my girls. I
brought them home last night, fed them dinner, put them
to bed, and now it is morning. Sunday morning. I am back
among the clutter and the wreckage. Oh God.

And here it is.

After walking and drinking and Zumba-ing and hydrating
and getting together with girlfriends and shopping and fighting and divorcing and kissing and going to therapy and pray-
ing and playing Solitaire and sometimes allowing it to overflow
but most of the time staving it off by running out ahead of it,
driving out ahead of it if necessary, in the freeway's diamond
lane, and then getting a new water bottle and buying new running shoes to dance as fast as one can to keep it from coming
down . . .

It comes down.

This is no longer a mere purse of anxiety that sits on the
chest, it's like my open coffin already ten feet down, as the dirt

slowly, like sand in an hourglass, begins to pile in on me. The sunlight hurts. My body hurts. The visuals of the bedroom hurt, the burnt-tangerine walls, the piles of clothing, the dusty books. Just blinking my eyes hurts.

It's 8:17 on a Sunday morning, the day is already too long, and tomorrow will be another day, and another, and another. All upcoming projects represent huge downward-plunging daggers of anxiety; every household task undone (ants, dishes, recycling) is an accusation; the upswell of the heart of love is gone, love has washed out, love is never to return, what is left are chores.

My heart hurts. I am hyperventilating. The four corners of the bed are tipping. There is more and more noise pounding in my ears. I can't outrun it. It is overtaking me. I have blown up my life.

All I can do is lie still.

I can hear the children puttering in their bedrooms. It's Sunday. Sunday morning. I should make breakfast for them and inquire after them, how they slept, and send them down to the piano and make sure they are doing their homework, so they don't just languish in their jumbled rooms all day. There is also laundry to be done and sorted, either by me or I need to reconceive it into some elaborate game. Should I take them to the Huntington, to the Huntington Gardens, to walk and talk and look at plants? The sun hurts. The sun hurts my eyes. I can't move. When I move, the room appears to tip.

The more I listen to Hannah and Sally putter—the toilet flushes, one calls out to the other, the TV switches on—the more deathly afraid I become. I am afraid to be alone with

Hannah and Sally because I fear they will immediately read from my dull eyes what I can no longer hide—that I don't love them, never will again. That's the horrible secret at the core of this, the devil's sibilant whisper. At one time the sweet smell of baby Hannah's head was my whole world; now I have lost that dreamlike forty-ish haze I was in during nursing and babyhood and toddlerhood, when the peach fuzz of my daughters' cheeks made for a heady narcotic, when my heart thrilled at all their colorful pieces of *kinder* art, when I honestly enjoyed—oh, the novelty, for someone who had pursued abstract subjects in college and graduate school for ten years!—baking birthday cakes. Almost fifty now, when I squat over to pick up their little socks and snip quesadillas into little bowls and yank fine hair out of their brushes, as I have now for the thousandth time, I feel as if I'm in a dream, but a very bad, very sour-scented dream. I have totally, finally, lost the will to continue this day job of motherhood.

There is a knock at the door. Hannah pokes her head in. She is in striped leggings and 3-D glasses, with her hair in a high, comedy ponytail, hovering with the Kindle. It's the matter of a two-dollar Kindle purchase. My eleven-year-old has slept in her bra. Her clothes are in a volcano on her dresser. She watercolors on her walls. The window won't close, so there are spiderwebs. If you look into her room, you would say she has no mother or no mother takes care of her.

I have nothing to offer her. All I say is: "Honey, come lie down next to me."

She obeys, and I wrap my arms around her and bury my

head in her neck. This is all I can do. I feel her weight. Then I start to cry.

"Uh-huh," she murmurs, stroking my hair. "I understand, Mommy."

What's curious is that I detect very little anxiety coming off her. In fact there is a sort of calm. Not just a calm, a sense of quiet theatrical importance around our moment together. Having been invited back into her mother's bed, where she dwelled on and off until the age of six, Hannah has a renewed sense of real estate. There is something deft about her hair stroking. It is not unlike the motion of brushing the hair of a Barbie or a stuffed unicorn. Poor baby. So confident. So clueless. What story can I tell her? "Honey," I say, "when I was a kid, my mommy had moods and she would literally disappear for three days, lying in bed, curtains drawn. And *nooo*body could get in. Nobody. Mommies had those kinds of moods back then. Very big stuff. Like when she—"

"Threw the glass Pyrex dish on her birthday," Hannah recites immediately.

I'm surprised. "I told you that?"

Hannah rolls her eyes. "About fourteen times! And about the butcher and her tennis skirts and the big amber jewelry . . ." Hannah rattles off my mother's story, and I am amazed at the fact that we're so close, we talk so much, and the boundaries are so invisible my daughter seems to know all my thoughts and memories, even the ones I forgot I told her.

But I know there are some things I haven't told her. After my mother hurled the Pyrex dish against the wall and disappeared into her bedroom like that tide washing out—door locked, curtains drawn, the thick silence—well, that was only the first time. What we didn't know then was that the highs would start waning, and what would eventually be the new normal was a fearsome long-term depression. The culmination was early Alzheimer's at fifty-nine and her death at sixty-nine. The last four years of her decline were so painful I didn't visit her in that horrible convalescent home, not once.

That's one gothic horror tale I don't have the heart to tell my daughter in this moment . . . but here is another. All these decades later, it is perhaps even more to the point.

Which is to say, my general experience with my mom was that even when that bedroom door closed and the silence fell, my mom was gettable, always eventually gettable. This was because I, her youngest, had learned a trick. I had learned how to break the spell.

Let us say we had all been planning to go to a fun neighbor's barbecue, of the sort my gregarious mother loved, but suddenly, an hour beforehand, my mother had shut down and taken to her bed. All you needed to do was take a deep breath, wedge yourself in, and sit—almost nonchalantly—on the edge of her bed, declaring, "Well, Mommy, if you are not going to the neighbor's barbecue, I'm not going either."

"What?" she'd say wanly.

Drop the head: "I'm too shy to go by myself."

And indeed, after a certain amount of pathetic-speak, the foam would form in the distance, the gurgling would begin, and the great tsunami of my mother would rise. She would get up and go to her closet and start coordinating an outfit, saying,

"Let's show them. Let's show them, you and I. Who do they think they are? We're *doing* it—I *insist*—we are *going* to that barbecue!"

But once I became a teen, the age Hannah is entering now, these gambits started working less and less. I remember one day after school, sitting down on the edge of my mother's dark bed and prattling on about some award I won that day or how a hated rival of mine bombed a test. The report was always about how I aced something and how my enemies fell. We thought this was the kind of story she liked. (As she said to my sister one day, excitedly, about a billboard she had seen: "When you put the 'oomph' behind 'try' you get 'tri-oomph'!")

Anyway, so there I sat wittily prattling on in a way I still do—I like to tease people with a bit of gossip, give them a little *amuse-bouche* of random detail, and then serve the main meal of it, the red meat encircled with garnish. I sat there wittily prattling—adding funny descriptions of wacky hair and what was said and what went wrong—and then I looked up, saw her dead eyes, and heard her say, "Mouseling? I'm sorry. I just don't care. I have things of my own to worry about."

The throwing of the Pyrex was nothing.

It was in that moment that something died.

When did she lose her will for all of it?

I remember my mother driving around in Brazil where, due to a university job of my father's, we lived for two years. I remember how she drove around aimlessly in the afternoons because she literally did not want to go back home to the dark, narrow student dorms (with monklike single beds in a row) where my cheapskate-to-the-death dad insisted we live. My father stamped out her spirit, again and again. There was no escape for her. She had no workplace, or mortgage of her own, or a Mr. Y. She did not even have Judith's house on Sunswept to visit. She had only the car, and the empty rainy streets. I feel so badly for her. I feel her sadness so deeply. I miss my mother so terribly, like a hole in my heart. . . .

And I feel rage that *he* is still alive! *Why! Why? Why?*

Why does the grotesque live, dragging us down? Why does he live on like a wizened diapered baby while my mother has been dead already for so many years? Why did I need to face adulthood without a mother?

I remember when my kitten got run over. My mother was devastated. She put it in a green garbage bag and cried and cried. She said she couldn't stop picturing that little cat. Just as I couldn't stop picturing poor Hammy the Hamster. Tumbling and tumbling and tumbling.

"We know you're not feeling well, Mom," Hannah says, turning elegantly, balletically, to pick something up from the nightstand. "So I made you a card." She opens it for me. It reads:

Dear Mommy,
   Get Well Soon.
   You work so hard,
   You need a break,
   You have more stress,
   Than we could take,
   So just shut your eyes,
   Lie down, relax,

Dear Mommy

Get Well Soon...

You work so hard,
You need a break,
You have more stress,
Than we could take,
So just shut your eyes,
Lie down, relax,
Throw ~~around~~ around money
Who gives a sh☺t about tax?

I ♥ UNDERSTAND AND FOREVER
LOVE, Your
♥ -Hannah

Throw around money,
Who gives a shit about tax?
I UNDERSTAND AND FOREVER
LOVE You!
Hannah!!!

"Is this from . . . the three-hole-punch-paper packet? In the cabinet?" I ask. "That I bought for that project I'm working on?"

Hannah pauses, guarded, like a deer at a water hole.

"Oh never mind, honey," I say, taking her hand. "Thank you."

Then I turn over and cry.

The next gambit is breakfast. The girls decide they will bring me breakfast. Not hungry at all, I obediently hobble downstairs like an invalid and sit on the porch on the outdoor chaise, like a muffin, under my comforter. I know there is a bit of self-interest here: My girls wait for any opportunity to invade the kitchen and start a huge messy project—cookies, lemonade, cupcakes, Depressed Mother Special Breakfast. The ants, however—just as Mr. Y predicted—are gone. The teeny-tiny armies of darkness have gone home.

Sally comes out as a waiter (sweatshirt around waist) and presents my feast. First comes her special scrambled eggs with cinnamon, pumpkin-pie spice, basil, and what appears to be a little bit of orange. It is not delicious. Here comes another moment of despair. Ever since I let the girls and their cousins perform "Sliced" (a kid version of the cooking show *Chopped*) in my kitchen, where some of our "found" ingredients included canned pineapple and stale mini-marshmallows and expired

Ricola cough drops (which actually got grated into a burrito), very strange cooking things have begun to occur. It is yet another example of how I have let the horses run out of the barn on this whole parenting thing.

And yet I think of Judith's coffee rule. You must transcend your actual candid response to the food, and just appreciate the gift of being brought it. I pretend to enjoy some and Sally beams.

I GO lie in Sally's large bed in her room, which, due to a cable logistical snafu, in fact holds our house's only TV. *SpongeBob SquarePants* is on, but not too loud, so it is passable. Sally is crocheting. Hannah is Kindle-ing. I am trying to look at an article I am working on, but can't for the life of me focus. Eventually I just put it aside and stare up at the sunlight on the ceiling. I invade my daughters' space by insisting on grabbing an arm of one and circling my ankle around that of another and this feels good. My heart-pounding lessens somewhat.

I remember when they were toddlers and we would lie together in the king bed back in the old house in the afternoon in the sun. Or at night, when sometimes I would sleep across the bottom of the bed, which is the absolute best place on the bed, it is like a totally new mattress because no one goes there, and I would feel complete, like a great universal zero with two Xs on me keeping me securely moored and on earth.

I start to sense, amid the gray, flecks and darts of warm color flitting through the air above me. I am trying to grasp at what they are and trying to articulate them. I realize, as the light lightens somewhat, that I have memories of some real pleasures. I am confessing things to my girls, in half-bitten-off sentences that don't even make any sense.

"Oh honeys, I know this sounds weird, but I remember how I used to actually kind of enjoy breast-feeding you—"

"*Eeew*," they both say.

"Oh kids, come on."

What I mean—but don't say—was that there was a time when an inestimably rich atomic soup of hormones was swimming, when I was young, when love was grand and large and easy, and I had a small earth-smelling creature and my only job was to keep feeding it. You could lie in a sunny bed in an afternoon, hook the small fluffy head into your body, have a beer even, and not give a worry about work or laundry or e-mail or for that matter, even dinner. There is this time during babydom that the mother herself can lie about like a baby, like a beached whale, having birthed her bloody spawn, and the mother can just hover in those sparkling dust motes of afternoon sun and be cradled and lifted and suspended in the golden light.

"Oh don't worry—it was just kind of a hormonal thing," is what I finally say.

"Nonetheless there will be no breast-feeding today," says Hannah firmly, and this strikes us all as funny. I snuggle back into her side, hard.

We spend the rest of the day in bed watching television. In the early afternoon something magical happens. Our favorite demon show comes on. "Oh God! *Mustard Pancakes!*" they scream. "Mom! There it is! A totem from our wretched childhood!" Indeed it is: It is a now-amusing nostalgic memory from their grotesque toddler years of being pulled across Target parking lots and peeing on car seats and hurling Skeeballs at Chuck E. Cheeses. It is from a time when, while single-parenting, I let my daughters watch as much television as hospital patients in full-body casts. "This really is a very bad show," I agree. "It's like dirty sock puppets." We also eat and make buckets of popcorn—butter, salt, no apologies. It's amazing how deeply relaxing bad habits can be.

"If my mom had only had a television in her bedroom!" I half joke.

IN THE morning at six fifteen I am resigned to my day but not actually incapacitated. I am regretfully pouring my coffee into its ridiculously cute mug and smearing PB and J on a bagel. Which is to say it is Monday morning at six fifteen, and for some godforsaken and unbelievable reason I feel . . . okay. Let's say the word slowly, as if to preschoolers: *O-o-o-k-a-y!* I don't feel great, but I am functional. I wait for it to come down, but it does not come down.

I am startled by Hannah appearing suddenly behind me. This is unusual—usually she waits upstairs for me to bring breakfast. Hannah puts her arms around me and kisses me on the nose. She makes some shy but insistent *wuvvy-wuvvy-wuvvy* sounds.

"Oh God," I say. "Here you are kissing your mommy on her *wuvvy-wuvvy* nose. I feel absolutely pathetic."

We laugh.

Driving to school, it appears we are going to be late, I am slaloming through traffic, and now Sally is starting to make high-pitched panic sounds because I haven't filled out her emergency form. I declare loudly that we will not have panic. We will not have panic. "We won't have panic over the emergency form!" I yell, feeling a rise of panic.

"Sally, it will be fine," Hannah says quickly and firmly to her sister, and in that moment I see a flash of something I've never seen before. It is the unguarded, careful, even slightly frightened face of the wary older daughter, keeping the other children in line, but maintaining a light, studiedly casual sing-song as she does so. Because Mother is fragile, and I am her ward, even responsibility, Hannah is patrolling the perimeter.

When I was in my teens I was sleepwalking, with myself at the center of my world, and everyone else as minor characters—that's how for granted I took my mother. And so I don't remember exactly when my formerly charming, humorous, omnipotent mother, who would swim a mile out into the ocean to get your beach ball in choppy seas, did the great recede. But like a tide gradually but irrevocably washing out, she retreated, she receded, she drifted away, and there was nothing anybody could do about it.

Why?

I'm not a great reporter on this because, being the younger, I feel I don't have firsthand information. There are unique memories my older sister, the firstborn, still holds—bedroom conversations they had, and harsh instructions that only she was privy to. I was the younger, but a lowly private marching in the losing desperado mission that was my family.

All I know is that my mother did recede. And as in so many cases, there is a child standing on a shore and watching her mother recede.

Fighting to stay in the game, I feel very conscious of my daughter's heart vibrating in front of me, absolutely exposed and without defenses. She has an openness of heart, a purity of intention, and the absolute belief that at eleven years old she can change the dictates of fate. Her eleven-year-old heart is like a golden egg trembling in a spoon I hold in front of me.

I want to keep this egg safe. Keep it safe.

Dinner at Home

I HAVE TO SWING BY Judith's in the afternoon to pick up a duffel bag of clothes I mistakenly (or perhaps not so mistakenly) left behind. My children are back at their dad's. It is with a heavy heart that I turn home, just before dusk. I have not bought any groceries for dinner. The night looms ahead.

But when I pull back into the crunchy gravel of the driveway, the doors are open, lights are on, jazz is playing, and I can smell something wonderfully garlicky cooking.

I mount the steps to the back-porch door, put down my duffel bag. In crisp shirt and chef's apron, Mr. Y comes immediately toward me, takes my face in his hands, and says, "How are you, honey? I missed you."

He looks good and smells good and fits me as naturally as a glove, as I do him. As usual, I don't even recall what we were fighting about, except it was all shadow puppets on the wall and, as always, to the death.

I sink into his chest and touch his hair. "I missed you too."

Inside I see the house has been cleaned and put back together.

There are fresh flowers everywhere, packed-up cardboard boxes where Mr. Y's nests used to be, and fresh candlesticks waiting with new candles. It's such wonderful middle-aged woman's soft porn.

He pours me a glass of wine, and we have an elegant and delicious dinner that feels like coming back home again. We have sorely missed talking with each other, and missed the bonhomie and actual friendship we used to have before the Desert Storm days came down. We are able, once again, to talk vividly and yet noncombatively, catching each other up on a panoply of subjects, happenings, and gossip. We are actually even able to talk about *Jam City*, which just finally closed, which I had seen three times after all during its run. Oh yes I had, even though I am a narcissistic diva with no interest in anyone's work, although I did have some notes—as usual, I always have notes—but he graciously acknowledged that they were good notes, and that in certain cases he had thought the same thing.

After dinner he insists he will clear the dishes. But first he goes upstairs and draws a bath for me, into which he shakes lavender. He puts on Bill Evans on Pandora, which he knows I love, and lights candles.

But no.

This was a dream.

But—yes!—it *wasn't* a dream. It was real! Because in fact this is the sort of magic Mr. Y pulls off easily when he has it in mind to do it, which generally is fairly often. It's a sort of beautiful and civilized domesticity that I miss when he leaves.

But I have it today and am grateful.

"Thank you," I keep saying. "Thank you. Thank you."

As surprised as I am when he takes a job, I am always just as surprised when it ends. I always have this feeling that he is going to go there and sit in the darkened theater regardless, but in fact, no; when it's over he stops going—he comes home and picks up his *New York Times* again. And things are as they were.

IT'S NOT enough, however.

When I wake up in the morning, even though we are in our usual tangle with our arms around each other and weight against each other under our warm blankets, the familiar gray light comes through the windows, and I feel the heaviness come down. *It* is still here.

"Oh no, not again!" I cry out in despair.

Mr. Y's presence is not enough to cobble everything over. There is such darkness.

I start to sob. I'm happy he is here, I guess, but everyone is just too intense for me. It's all just too much weight to drag forward.

"What do you need, honey?" he asks. "What's wrong?"

That gray light: I hate that gray morning light.

Dr. Valerie

I FINALLY SURRENDER AND GO for estrogen replacement to Ann's dream gynecologist, Dr. Valerie. Although Dr. Valerie is *not* in my Anthem Blue Cross PPO plan, Mr. Y insists I go to her anyway. In fact he drives me himself. After a series of tearful, incoherent conversations when I tell him I can't possibly go because I'm afraid to be weighed, he simply puts me—still weeping—into the car, and takes me to the doctor. It's another thing straight men do well.

A nurse opens the door of the waiting room and says, "Sandra?" I go in, get on the scale, it's a horrible number. But then the nurse frowns at her clipboard and says, "Sarah? I'm sorry—no, I meant Sarah, not Sandra." So I go back into the waiting room, cry a bit more, thinking at least I'm losing water weight. Five minutes later another nurse calls me. She puts me on that same scale again and I am not kidding, I am actually a pound and a half heavier.

I just cry harder. And clearly just by that very act am putting on more weight. Jesus. I cry and gain weight and don't even have to eat anything. My tears are actually making fat.

But Dr. Valerie has been worth—well—a year's wait.

With kind cornflower-blue eyes and a comfortingly patterned knit cardigan, exuding an air that you might expect from a Scandinavian maiden aunt, Dr. Valerie gently interviews me—while continually handing me tissues—as I sit on that archetypal metal table, finally, in my own paper gown, weeping for what seems like an hour. I describe all of it, the infinite varieties, colors, and shades of my depression, the gloomlets, the darkies, the panic attacks (going heavy to light, light to heavy, heavy to light), the whole horrible fucking mess.

Dr. Valerie, listening quietly, writes down the dates of my periods on a tablet, lending my ravings a reassuring scientific structure. And then she gives me one of the most deeply comforting speeches I have ever heard (who from central casting would you get to do it? Streep? Mirren? Lansbury?):

"Sandra," Dr. Valerie says, "I have this theory. Let me see if I can describe it for you. I think some girls are paper-plate girls, and some are Chinets. Paper plates collapse even if they have nothing on them; Chinets can take a lot heaped on them and never break. Yes, right now things feel very unstable, and you're having an emotional response to what is a purely physiological phenomenon. But I think, at heart"—and here she leans forward—"you're a Chinet girl. What we'd like to do now is take some of the stressors off your plate, while at the same time temporarily strengthening its foundation."

And with that she gently smears the tiniest dot of clear estrogen gel on the inside of my wrist. Even though she had said it would take a few weeks to take effect, I instantly feel better, almost even a little bit high. Although, to be quite frank, I also loved her handing me the tissues, patting me on the knee, and saying, "There, there."

I'M NOT saying the rest of the year was perfect, good, or even happy by any means. But a little bit more of it shifted from somewhat darker to somewhat lighter, and that balance helped.

I also did start practicing some of Mr. Y's New Age breathing, and started to force myself to say aloud phrases like "All will be well" and "I feel okay." And sometimes I actually found that it tipped the balance forward and actually worked!

I didn't end up using the estrogen gel for longer than three months, but I loved having it. I'm happy to have it in my bathroom drawer like insurance.

A more regular housecleaner also did wonders.

The Wisdom of Menopause

So what did I learn in this year?

Arguably, I learned that perhaps if I had stopped protesting too much and gone to the doctor (rather than just a therapist) earlier, I could have—somewhat—ameliorated a few months of grief.

Arguably also, I could have gotten a bit more of a handle on what was going on if I had read a really fantastic book on menopause—one that wasn't only about hormones or only about therapy, but something that combined both.

And never mind all my earlier quibbling about menopause literature, I did finally discover one totally helpful book, a classic that rises like a Mount Etna above the rest. The wonderful Dr. Valerie recommended it to me. The book subsequently became my own personal Dr. Valerie (a doctor to whom, oddly, I never felt I needed to return, although I think about her often, which in my mind only deepens her mystical quality).

The problem, of course, is that this magical book is 656

pages long, which can be extremely challenging for middle-aged women struggling to concentrate. So as a public service to the planet, let me try to convey its essence to you.

More than ten years old, *The Wisdom of Menopause*, by Christiane Northrup, MD, is the literal bible of middle-aged womanhood. After spending forty (seventy? one hundred?) hours with it, I've come to believe that *The Wisdom of Menopause* is an actual masterwork. Weighing more than two pounds, it is an astonishingly complete, mind-bogglingly detailed orrery of the achingly complex, wheels-and-dials-filled Ptolemaic universe that is womanhood. Featuring, archconventionally, its smiling doctor-author on a soothing pastel cover, the book is very much of the genre, and yet explodes it. About three times as big as any other menopause book, *Wisdom* is no less than the Jupiter in the menopause-book solar system, our *Gravity's Rainbow* or *Infinite Jest* (eat nothing but zero-calorie noodles and gain seven pounds? Ho ho ho! Infinite Jest!).

ARE YOU grasping, yet, the scope of this thing? (I'm sorry—just treated myself to a bit of estrogen gel—am really excited.) *Wisdom* is a Homeric poem of modern womanhood. No stone from Western or Eastern (or Southern or Northern) medicine is left unturned, from folic acid to breast exams to personal dancing to selenium to feng shui to cosmetic surgery (Northrup allows it, while counseling discretion as a protection against judgmental friends). She both delivers biological analyses of an almost kidney-squeezing complexity and boils them down to news you can use. For instance: "I highly recommend a snack at around four in the afternoon, right during the time when blood sugar, mood, and serotonin tend to plummet."

Doesn't that hit home? Although the Hour of the Wolf is typically considered to be four o'clock in the morning, for many mothers of school-age children, how many of our inner wolves appear at afternoon carpool time (4:00 p.m.)? This partly explains why many of us want to eat at five and why by "family dinner" at seven we want to kill someone—our family.

But what I really love is how passages on blood sugar and serotonin alternate with woo-woo passages on Motherpeace Tarot cards, and the chakra work of the astrologer Barbara Hand Clow.

That's right—I am not kidding. One of Dr. Northrup's sources is literally an astrologer. I do not rule my life by astrology, but I was curious enough to go to Amazon.com to order some of Barbara Hand Clow's seemingly oft-referenced work. Imagine my shock when I saw this—at least in my case—rather pointed title: *Liquid Light of Sex: Kundalini Rising at Mid-Life Crisis.* (As dubious as that title might sound, isn't it much more interesting than *The Happiness Project*? Sing? Clean out your closets? Oh please!) In it, she describes the Eastern mystical notion of kundalini rising.

Look, even if one is not a believer in chakras, on this I think we can all agree: From forty-five on, one can have a host of body ailments—from headaches to backaches to heart palpitations to gastric problems to fibroids to insomnia, and one can have a host of professional and relationship challenges going on at the same time. The seven chakras simply posit connections, say between jaw tenseness and blocked communication, or between lower-back issues and blocked creativity. (Northrup believes there's a connection between women who overworry and bladder issues—this actually describes 90 percent of the women I know. Neck and arm problems can be related to the heart chakra, which makes me think of my monstrous claw, an ailment I've never had before or since.) A typical Clow-type story is of a grieving empty nester having heart palpitations, for which she prescribes getting a puppy and lying down each day for an hour with that puppy on the sad person's chest. Instead of medication, a rescue puppy—who can quarrel with this? For myself, I found this chakra stuff folksy and sensible and interesting reading—I'm just generally more interested in stories about people's lives blowing up and how they put them back together than in a recipe book of a lot of low-fat menus involving flaxseed. Your results may vary.

I also enjoyed Clow's archaic astrological language involving the violence and upheaval of Saturn returns and Uranus returns and Chiron returns in seven- and fourteen- and nineteen-year cycles. (In her view, around age twenty-nine is a major passage, as is around age fifty.) I've seen many women (and men, whom Clow's book also refers to) go through real volatility in midlife, involving wild larger-than-life emotions and drives and imbalances that I think truly cannot be solved by date night, a beach vacation for two, or even more regular maid service. (Or you can do those things to keep up appearances but lead an entirely secret life on the side, and lie.) From forty on, I myself felt less like I was having some minor emotional issues and more like I was going through some kind of deep cosmic disturbance, something very old and molecular and primal.

HOWEVER, AS I suggested, even under my inspiring leadership, it is unlikely that the targeted demographic of women will ever engage in Bloomsday-like readings of *Wisdom*, as is done with Joyce's *Ulysses*. (Groused a girlfriend to whom I was maniacally recommending it: "Why should I bother? Every day of menopause *already* feels like you're reading a six-hundred-page book.")

So, for the bloated and tired, let me give you the juicy core. Writes Dr. Northrup:

A woman once told me that when her mother was approaching the age of menopause, her father sat the whole family down and said, "Kids, your mother may be going through some changes now, and I want you to be prepared. Your uncle Ralph told me that when your aunt Carol went through the change, she threw a leg of lamb right out the window!"

Although this story fits beautifully into the stereotype of the "crazy" menopausal woman, it should not be overlooked that throwing the leg of lamb out the window may have been Aunt Carol's outward expression of the process going on within her soul: the reclaiming of herself. Perhaps it was her way of saying how tired she was of waiting on her family, of signaling to them that she was past the cook/chauffeur/dishwasher stage of life. For many women, if not most, part of this reclamation process includes getting in touch with anger and, perhaps, blowing up at loved ones for the first time.

Woo-woo! Duck, Uncle Ralph! Go, Aunt Carol! In short, never mind the complicated hormonal science, the wavy-graph technicalities of all those estrogen/progesterone/FSH fluctuations.

Opines the doctor: "I think it's useful to get your hormone levels tested. But it's far more useful to tune in to how you're feeling than to focus on a lab test, which gives, after all, just a single snapshot of an ever-changing process."

What the phrase "wisdom of menopause" stands for, in the end, is that, as the female body's egg-producing abilities and levels of estrogen and other reproductive hormones begin to wane, so does the hormonal cloud of our nurturing instincts. During this huge biological shift, our brain, temperament, and behaviors will begin to change—as then must, alarmingly, our relationships. As one Northrup chapter title tells it, "Menopause Puts Your Life Under a Microscope," and the message, painful as it is, is: "Grow . . . or die."

Put another way:

The old story of menopause was that the change was when a woman lost her fertility and her essence and her marbles. But in fact, as I have seen with my own tween girls, before girls start their periods they are just as self-centered and brash and annoying and farty as the next person, babbling on about their own crap, much like anyone else. But then the periods start, and it's all about boys, boys, boys, hair brushing to look cute for boys, boy bands, boy jeans, lipstick and eyeliner . . . and we lose them for a while to the cloud of fertility hormones, which makes them want to help people and serve people and cut up their sandwiches into ever-tinier squares.

Thirty years later, though, look who's back. Fifty-year-old Aunt Carol, throwing that leg of lamb right out the window. Because there never was a "real" Aunt Carol. It was only fertility's amped-up reproductive hormones that helped Aunt Carol thirty years ago to begin her mysterious automatic weekly ritual of roasting lamb just so and laying out twelve settings of silverware with an OCD-like attention to detail while cheerfully washing and folding and ironing the family laundry. No normal person would do that—look at the rest of the family: They are reading the paper and lazing about like rational, sensible people. And now that Aunt Carol's hormonal cloud is finally wearing off, it's not a tragedy, or an abnormality, or her going crazy—it just means she can rejoin the rest of the human race: She can be the same selfish, nonnurturing, nonbonding type of person everyone else is. (And so what if get-well casseroles won't get baked, PTAs will collapse, and in-laws will go for decades without being sent a single greeting card? Paging Aunt Carol! The *old* Aunt Carol!)

Do you see? If, in an eighty-year life span, a female is fertile for about twenty-five years (let's call it ages fifteen to forty), it is not menopause that triggers the mind-altering and hormone-altering variation; the hormonal "disturbance" is actually fertility. *Fertility is the change.* It is during fertility that a female loses herself, and enters that cloud overly rich in estrogen. Due to life spans being as long as they are, thirty years of addled fertility in the middle isn't the "norm" for a woman, that almost sixty years of the relative selfishness of prepubescence and menopause are.

In short, if it comes at the right time, menopause *is* wisdom. For Northrup—whose own passage through menopause included a traumatic divorce, a narrative she relates with sadness but finally no regrets—this seemed to be so. In Northrup's generation, menopause's liberating narrative dovetailed elegantly with a typical female baby boomer's biological and chronological clock. When a woman gets married in her twenties, has children in her late twenties or early thirties, and begins to detach in her forties, look where her nuclear family is by the time she reaches her menopausal-wanderlust-filled fifties: Her grown-up (say eighteen-year-old) children are leaving the nest; her perhaps slightly older (say sixty-ish) husband is transitioning into gardening and fishing; her aged parents have conveniently died (let's say back—and wouldn't it be lovely?—when they slipped and injured a hip at, oh, seventy-eight).

Compare that timeline, however, with the clock of my own generation of late-boomer/Gen X women. Putting our careers and ourselves first, we adventured and traveled in our twenties, settled down and got married in our thirties, got pregnant (or tried to—fertility problems being the first surprising biological wall we hit) in our late thirties or even early forties. What scenario will *we* face when we hit menopause?

Oh my God! You've just witnessed it! Look at our parents! Owing to medical advancements, cancer deaths now peak at age sixty-five and kill off just 20 percent of older Americans, while deaths due to organ failure peak at about seventy-five and kill off just another 25 percent. So the norm for seniors is becoming a long-drawn-out death after eighty-five, requiring ever-increasing assistance for such simple daily activities as eating, bathing, and moving. This is currently the case for approximately 40 percent of Americans older than eighty-five, the country's fastest-growing demographic, which is projected to more than double by 2035, from about 5 million to 11.5 million. And at that point, here comes the next wave—77 million of the youngest baby boomers will be turning seventy. Move over Hurricane Courtney, here comes Hurricane Grandpa! Meanwhile, in terms of my children? In my case I have had the experience of combing lice out of my own wiry gray-and-white hair—a sobering sight one ideally wants to pair with nosebleed-high self-esteem, which few of us enjoy.

All of which is to say, how often have I felt, in midlife, as though I am in a strange Island of Doctor Moreau–like science experiment? My preteen daughters are flashing more and more midriff as they cavort to the gangsta rap of Radio Disney (PG or R? If I could only make out the *lyrics*!). My ridiculously old father is a giant baby who wheels his own crib into traffic, pees into a Starbucks cup, and still wields, intact, his own power of attorney. No wonder I'm feeling ever more sullen about it all; all gynecologists agree that at our age we should be living alone in a perimenopausal cave. It's not illogical to feel crazy. Oh no, feeling crazy is a reasonable reaction. Feeling crazy means you are being realistic about all that is on the Chinet plate.

What is not logical is to believe you can handle it if you keep spinning enough plates.

So who will supply all the caregiving when a whole sandwich generation of fifty-ish women checks out? Maybe it will be men.

I think, thank heaven, of Mr. X, my girls' fifty-something father, he who holds up the other end of the fifty-fifty custody balance beam. He is unfailingly calm and patient, buys them fashionable new jeans and tennies, braids their hair, punches new holes in their pink belts, takes them camping, cooks them baked beans, and butters their corn on the cob. By a natural chronology that doesn't imprison *him* in this Island of Doctor Moreau–like timeline—given that he would not have dreamed of wanting to do all this as a touring musician of twenty-five— my ex, I think, became a father at just the right stage, which is to say older. At his age, my girls have such a wonderfully nurturing father he might as well be a mother. And he is a better cook. And he teaches them discipline ("Get up on your feet, girl!"). And keeps their roof fixed. Thank God.

I think of a phalanx of us one time, standing in my father's dining room in Malibu, trying to figure out a schedule for his care—or at the very least for his capture. In the room at that moment were a failing Alice (seventy-two), myself (forty-nine), Filipino nurse number one (female, sixty), Filipino nurse number two (female, firty-nine), and Filipino nurse number three (male, forty-one). Which of us were going to take care of my dad? By the end essentially everyone had quit except for Thomas, the forty-one-year-old male, who alone has the strength to heft my dad's wheelchair in traffic, needs the money to support his own family of six, and is paid accordingly (which is to say well—far better than many young college graduates I know). Thank goodness his ring tone is so festive (I think my girls have set it to "Skater's Waltz") on my iPhone. Wherever it is.

POINT IS, the take-home from *The Wisdom of Menopause* is that rather than being a decline, due to increased longevity and improved health, this almost second half of our lives can be the best time of all. We can feel better, we can feel freer, we can feel clearer, and we can get more done in the world. Northrup believes that our hormones are literally rewiring our brains to get us ready to do this. As part of the process, "attending to our emotions is a crucial part of remaining healthy because the part of the brain that allows us to feel emotions has far richer and more complex connections with our internal organs, such as the heart and cardiovascular system, than does the area associated with logical, rational thought. . . . Your thoughts and your emotions affect every single hormone and cell in your body."

So now is the time to deal with all those old emotional memories/habits that have literally shaped your neural circuits. Fortunately, via "neuroplasticity," we can actually change our thoughts and emotional reflexes. Rather than endure panic attacks and fear and loneliness and anger and grief, it is interesting to start to think of some of these episodes as flooding hormones. Two in particular were interesting to me. Norepinephrine is the fight-or-flight hormone. "It makes your heart pound, blood rush to your heart and large muscle groups, your pupils widen, your brain sharpen." It gets you ready for battle, but if you withdraw adrenaline from your "account" too often, "you'll eventually be overdrawn." And then there's DHEA, or dehydroepiandrosterone, "produced by both adrenal glands and ovaries. . . . It helps neutralize cortisol's immune-suppressant effect. DHEA can actually be increased by focusing more on loving thoughts, loved ones, favorite pets, a delicious meal, a sweet memory."

In short, apparently your thoughts can direct your emotions and your physical responses. You can actually say things like "I am fine," and "All is well" in the middle of these panicky moments to bring your stress level down. You can change your thought patterns from dread into pleasant anticipation, depending on what end point you're fixing on. I guess that damned Eckhart Tolle was right—but I still reserve the right to absolutely abhor his papery T. S. Eliot "The Hollow Men" voice.

And dealing with the grief that we've been carrying for decades is the way to physical and emotional health.

But if all of that is too complicated, here, finally, is a fun way to think of it.

WISDOM OF MENOPAUSE ONE-SHEET:
MENOPAUSE AS LABOR

Christiane Northrup helpfully describes the various physical discomforts of perimenopause as "labor pain necessary for rebirth into happy, healthy, fulfilled" women ten years later. Rather than being a dethroned queen who is leaving the human race, you are pregnant with future potential, and what you're giving birth to is your next, *true* self.

She suggests you think of the giant, seemingly uncontrollable waves of emotion—from anger to depression to grief—as labor pains. They are completely natural, developmental, and in the end quite healing. You just need to keep breathing deeply and to let these waves wash over you with no judgment.

You can think of hot flashes in a similar, if slightly more complex, way. Dr. Joan Borysenko, the author of *A Woman's Book of Life: The Biology, Psychology, and Spirituality of the Feminine Life Cycle*, compares women experiencing hot flashes with Tibetan monks who follow a practice called tumo ("fierce woman") yoga. In tumo yoga the monks strip naked in freezing Himalayan caves, wrap themselves in wet sheets, and then miraculously dry the sheets via huge heat waves produced in their bodies through meditation. In consciously moving their internal life energy from their lower chakras up to their crowns, the monks believe they are burning away erroneous acts, wrong beliefs, and ego attachments.

So as middle-aged women we get to say how wonderful it is that our bodies are naturally doing that all day long! God (Tibetan?) knows we are busy multitasking, and perhaps do not have the air miles or time to go strip ourselves naked in a freezing cave in Tibet. What a lucky break! All this therapy is being done for us free of charge! Thank you, bloated, depressed, hotflashing body! Hurray!

Speaking of which, no one has mentioned bloating in this particular context, but I think it naturally follows. During much of my time in perimenopause, and frankly since—since the new "me" is experiencing a fairly long gestation, possibly similar to an elephant's—my middle has been so distended (even while literally fasting) it has felt as if I've been pregnant with a watermelon or baby walrus seal. But no, now I realize that fetus is myself. My belly is pregnant with myself!

So instead of being depressed about being bloated or trying to fight it too much, one can happily anticipate the new self who will one day arrive (perhaps when I am seventy-two, it seems). One is free to work on a new nursery for the baby or wonder what the new baby will look like. Will the new post-menopausal me be a happy if frizzle-haired lady in a house-coat with a mustache and three cats, and will she be called "Gladys?" Doesn't matter! I am feeling absolutely no panic whatsoever. *Ommm.*

I'm just delighted to be giving birth to a new self. A new self who will possibly need diapers, and that's all good!

In fact, why shouldn't we menopausal women contemplate throwing each other baby showers? We can register ourselves at As We Change and partake of festive party platters stocked with chocolates, wine, and Ambien (not the generic kind, the good kind—because we're worth it!).

I can't wait to see where the new me will end up going to college!

The Contents of My In-box

From Isabel:

I was recently told by my gyno (the wild and wacky Dr. Hamel Azarian) that I was no longer permitted usage of estrogen if I wasn't willing to add progesterone to the mix.

It had been so long (four years? five years?) since I first started ingesting estradiol pills, then switching to compound-pharmacy creams (the progesterone in that gentle form still gave me raging depression), I'd forgotten what it was like not to be continually dosed with estrogen.

It's been a month since I went cold turkey, and man! what a difference!

Of course there's a good news/bad news aspect, but for me the good far outweighs the bad.

Firstly (speaking of "weighs"), I lost 5 pounds of estrogen bloat that had been there so long, I figured that's what it's into now.

Without even thinking of cutting carbs, fat, whatever, FIVE POUNDS dropped.

That's the good news.

The bad news is continual hot flashes. And with the weight loss, I was convinced the flashing actually burned calories. But probably not.

However, things are becoming manageable with ESTRO-VEN MOOD AND MEMORY FORMULA! And I apologize for this e-mail starting to sound like an ad, but I'm totally in love with ESTROVEN MOOD AND MEMORY FORMULA!

Sure, I had difficulty recalling the word "refurbish" while telling Rich about our new neighbors and the house they're working to . . .

REFURBISH!

But I remembered it about a minute ago, thanks to ESTRO-VEN MOOD AND MEMORY FORMULA, and its amazing ginkgo biloba.

Plus there's tons of soy, and evening primrose, which does help with hot flashes. But, unfortunately, so does abstaining from wine (and coffee, which isn't going to happen either). However, a wine/caffeine flash is fleeting, once on the ESTRO-VEN MOOD AND MEMORY FORMULA regimen.

I'm seeing light at the end of the tunnel. I am 170 days from being officially pronounced menopausal, and like my friend Jan, I expect to "dance a fucking jig" to commemorate it.

Hope you're well.

Love,

I

From Kaitlin:

Papa walking. Next on water. . . .

From Thomas Flores:

hello boss,

just letting you know that everything is fine with FLORES
team. eugene is ok and able to walk again. we have 5 days
straight schedule in wise.i just hold lexapro pill since it was
prescribe for he is ok and very cooperative with me. anyway
thanks for trusting us and we do hope that everything will be ok
again for this week.by the way if you have time pls. make my
deposit tom or wed.(aug 21 or 22) instead on thurs.(aug.23), I
made check dated wed and im worried about bank charges.
thank you so much.best regards . . .

Thomas

From Kaitlin:

PS. Even if it's not true about Papa walking again and even
if he isn't even alive anymore (aka: *Weekend at Bernie's*) isn't it
awesome to get these wonderful e-mails from Thomas?

Turning Fifty

I ADMIT THAT I'M NOT that thrilled about turning fifty. My instinct is not quite avoidance, but it is to do something very, very low-key. I'm thinking less "celebration" than a kind of subtle holistic offstage underwater birthing . . . ceremony. In Australia.

No. In reality, my idea is to mark this passage with a quiet champagne potluck for perhaps a dozen women friends. I am thinking lots of soft cheeses, and many stunningly expensive little chocolates—of the gourmet kind that invoke sea salt, lavender, rose hips, etc. Our Wiccan circle could dine and share stories and toast the fabulousness of fifty, with many inspiring affirmations (taken from books like *Women Who Run with the Wolves* or *When I Am an Old Woman I Shall Wear Purple*). We could then write down things we wanted to get rid of and throw those pieces of paper into the fire (a thing I had never in fact managed to do at Burning Man).

Unfortunately, my fiftieth birthday actually falls on a Saturday, which seems to give the lie to slipping on quietly through the night with cheeses, food that I no longer absolutely deny myself anyway, now that I've given up on my Spartan lifestyle. (What happened was that I had a lucky score at Ross Dress for Less, where I got a few pairs of magical "mom" jeans, on sale. They are in regular-sounding sizes but have tons of room and are all made of stretchy fabric. I feel oddly newly comfortable and stylish, at least for me. Ross Dress for Less!)

No, Saturday night is calling for something big . . . Which makes me feel a bit sullen. Because it seems like I am always planning everyone else's party and no one is ever planning mine.

I have in fact, just pulled my bachelor composer friend Carlos's fiftieth birthday out of the fire. Literally two weeks before his birthday, he had sent out a plaintive e-mail that said, "I am turning fifty. Is there anyone who wants to offer their house for a party for me?" And of course being gregarious to a point of self-harm, I volunteered our house. But it was so last-minute that by the time Carlos had tweaked the Helvetica font one hundred times on the e-vite ("Carlos turns half of 100!") it was like five days before a Saturday, it was like in the nog-flooded middle of December, with all its Handel chorales and holiday office parties and daughters' *Nutcracker*s, so it looked as if we were only going to have six people out of thirty.

In order to avoid a lonely Stella Dallas bomb of an evening, I thought we should *joyously* and *festively* postpone the celebration to the empty weeks of January, but Carlos seemed to take my logistical strategizing the wrong way, and the next thing I saw was a mass e-mail copied to fifty people, titled: "CAR-

LOS' 50th BIRTHDAY CANCELLED BY SANDRA DUE TO LACK OF SUPPORT."

But in fact we did move it to January. And thanks to my strategic move, there was an upswell and crowd (more than fifty people!) and the wonderful testimonies that people tend to get together for people's fiftieth birthdays (in a way they don't quite deliver at people's fortieths). So, surprisingly, Carlos had the greatest and most touching fiftieth, and now here was mine, and I wouldn't even get as good a party as friggin' Carlos, because I didn't have myself to shill for me. I could really probably only get the twelve women. But maybe some of them could be drafted into bringing their reluctant husbands. Then I might get up to twenty people. I suppose that's a quorum.

So I am just typing the kind of pointed-if-vague "Save the Date" e-mail one needs to send out one month in advance when Mr. Y confesses that "something" has been planned that was supposed to be a surprise that he wasn't supposed to tell me about but perhaps now he should. I tell him very, very carefully and calmly I think that is wise. He confesses that Clare and a group of my girlfriends had already approached him five months ago about throwing a big surprise fiftieth birthday party for me. Clare had actually drafted three different invitation templates. But then Mr. Y had sort of let it drop through the holidays and all. But now that my birthday is four weeks away, maybe he should pick up the thread again and give her a shout-out.

You can imagine my immediate cortisol-flooding response. But given that Dr. Stacey is morbidly expensive and Mr. Y and

I are trying to live together again more harmoniously, I do my deep breathing. I repeat "All will be well," and . . . hit Send on my "Save the Date for MY SURPRISE PARTY I'M NOT SUP-POSED TO KNOW ANYTHING ABOUT THAT MR. Y IS SUPPOSEDLY COORDINATING."

I call Clare and tell her that, given the unfortunate lateness of the project's launch—particularly given that she started five months ago—trying to throw a big party is probably not a good idea. It's Saturday, it's Los Angeles, it's like setting oneself up to fail. Perhaps something smaller would be better, and throw in some lobster or something so the foodies would have to come (even though of course those tend to be the same people with season tickets to things).

"No, no, no, *no*!" Clare exclaims. "It's your fiftieth! You have to have a big party, an epic party! There's no argument! People will come! I will force them!"

"How?" I wail. "Everyone always has a million excuses—the traffic from the Westside alone! Think of Elise. You know what Elise is like. You'll invite her to my fiftieth birthday party and just get a monologue back about her allergies."

"Come on!" she says. "This is huge. If need be with Elise, I will tell her that you are in very, very fragile depressive mode and if she ever wants to see you alive again she needs to come and bring a very large gift. And that's the beauty of a surprise party, because then people can't bug you with phone calls begging off. It'll be much harder for them to diss me. I'm just waiting for Mr. Y to get me a guest list."

"Oh God, no!" I wail. Of the many things Mr. Y can do, putting together a thorough e-mail list of my friends with-

out my help is a super-Herculean task of which I believe few
heterosexual men are capable. They just don't have that gene.
"This means I'm going to have to do it! For my own surprise
birthday party!"

"Well, you'll do a much better job," Clare assures me. "Just
focus. Be shameless. Don't edit. Put on that list anyone you
can think of. Go far and wide. Include everyone—old boyfriends from high school you have dropped entirely, girlfriends
who became whiny and whose e-mails you actually stopped
responding to, an old work colleague who did you a professional
favor you never quite returned. Invite people you friended and
then whose 'feeds' you immediately unsubscribed to, invite
your fat friends, fat-friend new people and invite them, go to
town. Invite all your bosses—"

"Oh for Pete's sake—they'll never come! It's the last thing
they want—"

"But they may be shamed into sending you a gift! That's the
beauty! Because the next time they get an official announcement about you, you may be dead. Invite your financial adviser,
your mortgage broker, or anyone else who sends you a card
at Christmas. I must say how delightful it was the day before
my own fiftieth to sit on my doorstep and open a giant gift
basket—the full Monty, champagne, chocolate, cheese, spa
sandals—from Millie Olivas, my realtor from Dickson-Podley.
I had put so many fishing lines out there, it was a surprise
to pull up such a big fish on just one. But of course a realtor
always will send a gift, particularly a female realtor."

"You invited your realtor to your fiftieth birthday party?"

"Sure I did! Had I known it would work so well I would

have also invited my dentist, my gynecologist, and my newspaper carrier. Numbers, people, we want numbers!"

"This sounds awful," I say. "I just can't take the stress of this. And I'm going to be driving my dad around a lot this month. I simply cannot do this. No."

BUT THEN what happens is that I get tragic news about my friend Ray. Ray is one of my oldest friends, literally from college. As twenty-year-olds we used to grill things on a tiny outdoor hibachi in our dorm's courtyard and listen to music and talk about books. Ray has always had a wonderful optimism and sense of humor, and has gone on to have a successful career as an engineer in a beautiful part of Seattle. Or so I had surmised from his friendly annual Christmas letters, full of cheerful detail about hobbies (his was boating), his and his wife's two dogs, and wry commentary on the varying fortunes of his favorite sports team, the Seattle Mariners. You really couldn't have constructed a more normal, happy-looking life—they were always smiling on a mountain somewhere, or biking, or sailing, shading their eyes from the sun.

But no. Apparently Ray had been struggling with depression for the past ten years, and they couldn't quite get the mix of chemicals right. So he took himself out, and now after decades of e-mailing back and forth and sharing funny YouTube clips, now I'm finally flying to Seattle to see him, and he is in a coffin.

I admit that I am extremely pissed off at Ray. I am pissed off that he kept this stream of chat going (the Seattle Mariners? who the hell cares?) while he was so sad inside and could not

admit it, so he covered it up with all of this trivia. I am pissed
off that while women are accused—and perhaps rightfully—of
shrei-ing and kvetching and rapid-cycling and parsing, men
suffer many of the same depths and unpredictability of moods
we do, but they seem to do it alone, for fear of oversharing, and
it's a waste of life, literally.

I am very pissed off that by the time one hundred of Ray's
friends and relatives have gathered here in this small white
wooden church just outside Seattle to "celebrate" his life, he
isn't here to see it. Because maybe if he saw this church full
of people he might have staved off the darkness a bit longer,
because in point of fact we would have come flying if we had
known remotely how much he was suffering. I am pissed off
that I am the only friend from LA who flew in.

My black jacket and pants feel too tight, and my cheap
pumps are uncomfortable. The picturesque Norman Rockwell
quaintness of this church is suffocating and discordant.

Why is the organist playing "Amazing Grace"? It has nothing to do with Ray. He was into Steely Dan, Emerson, Lake &
Palmer, Berlioz. I look around around at the rows of wooden
pews. Why are so many smiling white-haired elders of the
church here, and so few of his same-aged friends?

The reception afterward takes place on a manicured rect-
angle of lawn overlooking an unusually and cruelly sunny
Puget Sound. There is a buffet of roast-beef sandwiches and a
tray of cookies and coffee, caf and decaf. It is the saddest kind
of adult "mixer." I meet a long-ago woman friend from Ray's
junior-college days thirty-five years ago. She is not technically
an ex-girlfriend, but by the carefully preserved photo-booth

photos and neat collection of handwritten notes they had exchanged, one sensed maybe she would like to have been. She is a fourth-grade teacher from Tacoma with a gray ponytail and wide hopeful eyes, who I think, thirty-five years later, is still in love with him.

Because it is a church "celebration," no mention is made of Ray's depression or of his suicide, only of his love for his (now-devastated, never-mentioned) wife and his dogs and his boat. And the fucking Seattle Mariners. The long-ago woman friend—Darlene—is continuing to follow suit.

"Ray was so funny! He was so literate! And so brilliant, so brilliant. What a wonderful ceremony. It was so fun to hear those old childhood stories about him." And then Darlene adds a quietly bewildered afterthought: "I—did you?—I had no idea he was in such a bad state."

I put my paper plate of roast beef down.

"Darlene?" I say candidly, as she is the only person in Seattle I have to talk to. "I think it's a shame people don't talk about moods more. I believe that difficulty coping with ordinary life is more common than we think. Maybe it's because we live in twenty-first-century America as opposed to eighteenth-century Ireland on a thundercloud-darkened heath. We just don't seem to have any vernacular for addressing some ordinary garden-variety darkness. In the newspaper, there is a crossword puzzle and a jumble and a sudoku and a KenKen but no Little Corner of Darkness with a melting scream face in it ('Find the Melting Scream Face. Level: Advanced')."

Encouraged by what I take to be her thoughtful silence, I continue. "I mean, just this last year I've been perimenopausal and I've had some real attacks of the darkies, some real winged monkeys coming after me. I've had days where just seeing the sharp early afternoon shadow a tree made by the side of the road would fill me with horrible despair, worse than an Edward Hopper painting—Edward Hopper, you know, who did *Nighthawks*. I guess it's like when the whole world becomes an Edward Hopper painting, with slightest greenish tints and too-sharp shadows and it is all corpses and mannequins and wax figures and it's all about mortality and everything is death. But no longer is it just a lonely city coffee shop at midnight, but this is what everything previously comforting now looks like: spring, Christmas, shortcakes, parks, a hazelnut latte, muffins, children, puppies, bunnies."

"Nice meeting you," Darlene says, gathering her mementos, moving away.

Ah well.

KAITLIN AND I will end up throwing my father a blow-out ninetieth at the Malibu Beach Club, where amazingly a big festive crowd turns out, not irritated at their neighborhood eccentric but in fact, more and more as the years have passed, affectionate fans. They've taken a certain familial care of my dad ("Oh yeah, I've always given him rides to the bus stop") as you would a wryly beloved tidepool treasure. Surprising guest? I kid you not—Ricky Jones, a skateboard dude whom I distinctly recall being a pal of Sean Penn's at hideous Malibu Park Junior High, his overhanging cloud of surfer hair now graying. Apparently even he is a longtime fan of my father. "I remember waking up in the sand hungover in the summer and Mr. Loh would say, 'Merry Christmas! Merry Christmas!' Your dad! The wacky professor! What an awesome guy!"

My father is a bastard but you only turn ninety once. Thank God. The party and wacky beach people testimonials were completely hilarious and perfect.

I saw how everyone is under orders now to throw everyone else parties for the big ones, because if you don't, people will gather only at your memorial and that is a waste of life.

A great party, however, everyone can remember.

Your fiftieth birthday party is the one last event in your life, after your wedding, if you've had one before then, where friends, family, and acquaintances can be guilted into showing up, and they can be guilted into bringing a gift, even if it's a joke gift. A fiftieth birthday is the half-century mark. It is imbued with both festivity and gravitas. By this point everyone knows plenty of people who didn't make it to fifty, and everyone knows plenty of people who are at least twice divorced, so showing up is not just a pledge to the guest of honor but a pledge to all of our mortality. There's no other event like it in the life cycle. Jewish kids have bar and bat mitzvahs, of course, but these events celebrate kids who have actually lived only thirteen years. No, the only event like a fiftieth birthday–the only event that celebrates and commemorates you as a grown-up, with a full, adult life, will be your funeral. So let this celebration of your fully golden self happen when you are alive. And have some cake, for God's sake.

. . .

so i compose the opus of my e-mail list, Clare sends it out, and within days Mr. Y tells me, unbelievably, that we are expecting 150 people. I won't lie—it makes me feel fantastic. I love a big party. I can't wait.

So the day of my fiftieth opens with the kids and Mr. Y bringing me breakfast in bed—applesauce with Cajun seasoning on an egg. Oh well, regardless of the strangeness of my breakfast, it was made with love, and today is going to be a wonderful day because all I am doing is working on my killer fiftieth-birthday-party dance mix. I've bought a brand-new iPod touch and have just learned how to download music and make playlists, and I am completely engrossed in this project. I finally have a hobby! I am one of those magical people who can happily while away a day without drawing hash marks on a page and penciling them in (Shades of Grey)! Yayyy!

But it's even bigger than that. The fact is, I have lived half a century to create the amazing legacy of this historically unprecedented dance mix. I will make it into an app. I will be famous among my grandchildren! I will be elected *Time*'s Person of the Year!

"And what is your dance mix?" Mr. Y asks indulgently, from behind his *New York Times*.

"All right," I say. "Thank you for asking. You can ignore me completely as I speak, as you usually do while reading. I believe all of dance begins and ends quite simply with the Commodores' 'Brick House.' It's all about 'Brick House.' It's basically a five-hour plan for easing not 'Down the Road' but into, and out of, the Commodores' 'Brick House.'"

"Aha," he says.

"I realize I may seem a bit manic here, but I am excited. Let me tell you how it goes. We begin with the Motown/oh-hello-old-friend-sitting-at-the-bar-and-finishing-your-drink section, prompting the gentle swaying in the chair, the refreshing of the beer, the final trip to the bathroom to fix the lipstick. Then it's Wilson Pickett, Aretha Franklin, early James Brown, Marvin Gaye's 'Grapevine,' Stevie Wonder's 'I Wish.' It's the sound track to the Big Chill section, perhaps somewhat cliché, but comforting and familiar. People need to have had at least two beers, perhaps three, before loosening up. It is at this exact moment now that the party gauntlet is thrown down, hard, with the Jackson Five's 'ABC' and then—yes, people—even some disco. We are talking 'Funkytown,' 'Freak Out!' and even 'Boogie Shoes,' just for laughs. And now—*doot! doot!*—the Michael Jackson train pulls into the station, starting with 'Gonna Get it Started,' 'Thriller,' and—well, you see how many you can do before a panting Lily puts hands on hips and wails: 'Excuse me? Am I in some 1980s step class or what?' "

"*Oof*," he says. "Lily. Burning Man. Did she ever end up having that affair with the traveling LAUSD theater teacher?"

"No!" I exclaim. "He canceled the Indian dinner and did the big fade. The erotic e-mail was as far as it ever got."

"Well, that's kind of sad, but it's good too because I like Brian."

"We all do. Anyway," I continue, "it is at this point—end of hour two—where we throw in the towel and open the throttle wide with 'Brick House' and then 'Play That Funky Music White Boy'! Wow!

"Where can you go from there? Only one place—and here's

the turn! You have to change the palette entirely at this point, and the way you do that is with Latin! 'Oye Como Va' by Tito Puente. Now change of scene, shift of scene, it's a conga line through the house. Brazil and tequila will segue into another sweet sweet"—I do a Napoleon Dynamite hip flair—"dance hammock, 'Low Rider.' From there I may either go Stones and David Bowie or directly, depending on how gay the crowd, into *West Side Story* original Broadway cast version, 'One handed catch'!"

"Great!" he says, picking up the business section.

But in point of fact, for my girls this morning I have created a special tween dance mix ("Time Warp," "Jailhouse Rock," and even—well, you pretty much have to do it whether you want to or not—"Footloose"). Because it's my birthday and I can, I force my kids to audition my tween dance mix in my bedroom, and I realize that nine-year-old Sally does not try to conserve energy at all: She dances by jumping joyously into the air on every beat. Kids have not learned yet to contain their joy. They still have an endless supply.

We jump together to the young Michael Jackson, still so sweet and birdlike, still so classic, still so pure, it is like trampolining, and I realize that—fuck the gym and the machines and the grim torture of training and all those steel water bottles and all those rubber straps and CNN televisions. If I just dance every day with my girls the way they like to dance, no holds barred, I will get into the greatest shape of my life.

The whole day we clean up the house and cook food and I keep re-tweaking dance mixes, in my wonderful sunny home when the nests are (fairly) contained, armed with a core of people I dearly love. We move the furniture aside and these big wooden dance floors open and Hannah spontaneously breaks out into mad spinning and kicking and dancing. I do so love throwing a party. I am the sort of hostess who maniacally checks the RSVP list and tries to introduce compatible people to one another and to have snacks—not brilliant snacks, but enough snacks—and make sure there are plenty of festive beverages. Mr. Y grumbles that the guest list has become too large and he will have to move the cars and helm other burdensome logistics, but I know he is just being gruff for show because, like me, Mr. Y dearly loves a party, any party.

Mr. Y takes us out to dinner at an old-fashioned chophouse. Wonderfully, with that light buoying cloud lining of estrogen (coupled with a late afternoon snack of turkey and avocado, I'm not going to lie), I now have the capacity to sit with these three people over dinner and to actually converse with them. In fact, I feel so effortlessly bubbly and euphoric, I lead the group in a joke-telling session, which is quite unheard of. I turn it on and I have the girls in stitches, knowing them as well as I do. We don't just trade a blizzard of Tom Swifties like "The Yellow River, by I. P. Freely," "Spots on a Wall, by Who Flung Poo," and one I had never heard before, "African Lion Taming by Claude Mbuti," I even mention something funny about Burning Man, carefully framed, "Once we visited a camp in the desert that featured just a bunch of comfy chairs to rest in. It was called—and you have to say this very carefully, 'A Shack of Sit.'" The girls literally howl with laughter and declare that I am fun. I declare that they are fun.

And then Mr. Y begins to get anxious texts from Clare (who is at our house setting up).

He goes oddly silent.

It's then that I notice that the patter of rain on the roof has begun.

And oh no! Suddenly I know what is happening. It is Los Angeles, after all. Due to the drizzle we are going to get attrition, and instead of 150 people there will be 8 and I will be sorely disappointed and will spend the entire evening outside of myself, as I am so easily disappointed by everything in life. Oh God. Why am I like this? I wonder. I love fun so much that even sometimes in the middle of having fun, I get sad calculating at what point the fun will end.

Which is a long way of saying I am suddenly overwhelmed with sadness and horror and terror that I am walking into a birthday party *trap* where but a few hapless awkward souls will be and my children will see their mother destroyed. This was my very fear.

I feel that, as usual, too-optimistic-WASP Mr. Y probably wildly overestimated the numbers, particularly given the lateness of the invitation.

I feel like I'm going to an execution where once and for all it will be proved that *life is never enough* for me.

The cortisol starts firing. My throat starts closing. I am having a panic attack.

I have to excuse myself alone to get air in the parking lot, I am hyperventilating.

Mr. Y, tie askew, finds me in the parking lot. Amazed, "Get

yourself together," he orders me gruffly, pulling me toward the car, where the girls are already waiting.

In the confusion of Saturday-night traffic, we actually get home a tad late. It is quiet. There are very few cars out front. I start to whimper quietly and hate myself for doing so in front of my children in their fluffy party dresses.

But as we pull in, yes! There are strings of colorful party lights and a huge crowd spilling out everywhere. People have hats and bottles of beer and tacos, and as if in a dream or in a movie, in slow motion they are coming up and hugging me and laughing and spilling beer on me.

It is all these wonderful familiar faces—my sister, Kaitlin, my dad and his nurse, for God's sake, Clare, Ann, Isabel, Elise, Carlos and Judith and Roland. There are Burning Mom friends and their spouses and their children, as hale and tanned as if we were all camping in front of the capitol yesterday, although (can it be?) all the children seem several feet taller, and—oh God—there is Lily and her entire family, including their wonderful dog in a desert pirate bandanna, there are friends from grad school and college and even, oh my God, junior high. These are all the wonderful, wacky, crazy friends who have helped me through this year as I have helped or will help them. It's sort of like a This Is Your Life reunion.

Even my ex-graduate-school boyfriend, Ned—the one who preceded Mr. X—is there. I haven't seen him in seventeen years. Says he, candidly, as though he has been time-traveled in: "I literally have no idea how I got here."

I am immediately roasted—first of all for being late, due to my panic attack that no one was coming.

Says my fellow-nerd girlfriend Karen from Malibu Park Junior High School, with whom I was in the debate club (and who now runs a major animation division): "Even in junior-high school Sandra was deeply uncool, but Sandra has made a career out of it! Till I die, I am proud to remain a friend of a fellow survivor of two words: 'Jodi Schneekling'!"

Says my brilliant writer friend Janet: "Instead of running from fear, she moves toward pleasure." And it seems like such a graciously forgiving way of retelling my spotted life.

Even the cast of friggin' *Jam City* is there. They sing "Happy Birthday" a cappella, with a beat-box background, and they are actually so good I'm moved to tears. "I love those kids," I murmur to Mr. Y. "And SpookyZ can have that damned lamp."

And now of course the dance party unrolls. It turns out the living room is too crowded and the speakers aren't loud enough, so we put them up on side tables. We end up going not just through hour one and hour two but into hour three. After the Motown and disco and funk and Brazilian conga line with kids through the house, with Roland dancing bare-chested in white fur to Bowie, the dancing ends with myself and a couple of my deepest male-nerd friends (whom I have known since I was a nerdy teen in high school) braying the score of *West Side* story ("Maria! Maria!") until 3:30 A.M. At that point Mr. Y excuses himself to go for cigarettes and by accident locks himself on the balcony and has to pee over the side of the house and climb across the roof and break in via a window. It's a good big epic party.

The next day, I am actually late to my interview of Chelsea Handler for *MORE* magazine at the Chateau Marmont. It is the first time in my life I am late to interview a celebrity (or anyone else, for that matter). I am so beyond hungover and addled I simply cannot untangle the headphones on my tape recorder, so Chelsea Handler—a total professional—leans over and helps me untie them. Thus enabling me to think, on the second day of being fifty: Whew—thank God I'm with a person as sober and sensible as Chelsea Handler.

And indeed, as Clare promised, I am left with a pile of gifts from my friends and acquaintances and, face it, a few confused strangers who possibly had no recollection of what their relation was to me but who just showed up to be polite. There are pillar candles, liquor, champagne, lavender soaps, tapenades, blood-orange olive oil, and many, many gift certificates for massages. There are even, God love it, a couple of large hand-painted Italian platters, something I really miss from my days of marriage, those things I left scattered on the sidewalk in front of my faraway old hippie house in the mist, dammit. There is even a gift certificate for a wind tunnel that suspends you in midair called iFLY. It looks fabulous, and I will get around to using it one day, as well as to writing the thank-you card to Winnie.

It is indeed a kind of baby shower . . . for my new self.

I will need to rent a U-Haul storage unit just to store it all.

Old Lady Running

I'M WALKING ALONG THE Arroyo trail, something I do semiregularly now. I'm listening to the opening of *Petrushka*, "Shrovetide Fair," which is so lush it's like an extraordinary musical canvas deepening into color. The foliage smells good and the air is fresh and the world is full of light. Oh God, what a miracle, just to feel that, just to feel that.

What a gift just to be able to look out into nature and have this sense of deep okayness. Nothing is haunting me. There are no winged clawed things at my back. I just feel the sun and am okay.

Oh my God. I believe I am . . . fine.

I have, as usual, agreed with my girls to let tonight be Make Your Own Pizza. And I laugh. Because I have now acquired the wisdom to transform Make Your Own Pizza into Make Your Own (Damned) Pizza!

This switch was inspired by Christiane Northrup's story about wanting to skip putting up a Christmas tree when her kids were older, while also realizing she could reinstate the tradition as soon as they were willing to help her put it up, decorate it, and dismantle it. This is the important difference between caring, which is healthy, and overcaring, which is exhausting and manic. So not only do my kids cheerfully decorate and dismantle the Christmas tree every year—although I do make a point of carrying it over the porch myself, as I would my own bride (as I continue to try to become the man I want to marry)—they cut up all their own little "pizza" vegetables now with Costco Henckel knives, and they put all their own crap away, or at least most of it.

So we have converted Make Your Own Pizza into an enjoyable ritual that features me furtively yet joyously swiping generous amounts of shredded mozzarella, as is my right as queen of the kingdom, a new middle-aged pleasure I'm celebrating being that of stealing generous bites of my children's typically much-more-yummy food (macaroni and cheese, barbecue potato chips, Miracle Whip). Then we will stack my insanely colorful plates in the dishwasher and turn it on with a roar and will be done. The girls will get into their beds, lights will go off, I will do some abridged, updated version of a Beatrix Potter bedtime story—an abbreviation of their too-long childhood bedtime stories—and then I will snarl at them that it's enough already. I will go into the bath with a glass of wine and the good book I am reading. Mr. Y will try to coerce me into watching a Netflix movie with him on his tablet. I may agree. I may stay up too late and wake up cranky, but Thursday I have completely off. And all will be well.

It is a marvel to behold. It is a miracle. By changing my

thinking patterns, I have somehow become able to excrete a hormone that douses anxiety instead of fuels it.

And I've come to appreciate my tribal time alone. In spurts I am able to leave my village—Kaitlin and Ann and Isabel et al.—and spend time in my cave.

I am able to enjoy being alone, because I will see all those people again, soon, and everyone is fine.

Spontaneously—and this is unbelievable, I know—I break into a run. It's really a jog, but I call it a run. My exuberance takes me halfway up the next hill, at which point I realize the grade is really getting a lot steeper.

Uh-oh. It's suddenly an effort.

My legs ache. I have to bend my body forward practically in two.

I've never "run" in this position before. My feet keep moving, but seeing my crippled shadow, I think: Oh my God! I'm an old lady! This is the shuffling run of an old lady!

But then comes another voice (Streep? Lansbury? Mirren?). Call it the Hey, Chinet Girl voice. It pushes back at the gloomlet: Let's be real here. When were you ever a good runner anyway? You never ran! You never competed. Your life average has always been pretty much an eighteen-minute mile. You and Kaitlin used to do basketball layups that looked like small jetés. You have never remotely rocked as an athlete.

I remember also the shoulder and neck aches I used to have as a sixth-grader, due to my too-heavy backpack. The migraine headaches—they're the same exact ones I have today.

The fact is that I always worried. I always made to-do lists. Even at the age of eleven.

Then I think: Maybe I always was a fifty-year-old inside, and it was a matter of finally becoming my ideal age!

In fact, I now think about my performing-arts daughter, Hannah, and know for sure she is even less inclined to run—anywhere, ever—than I am. In fact, now that I think of it, my daughter always has the fifty-year-old-lady neck aches and always wants me to give her a back rub. And she is also always making to-do lists. In certain ways Hannah and I are developmentally the same age.

Nine-year-old Sally is not so far off either. Like me, Sally hates mornings—"I hate Monday!" she screamed recently, from under her covers.

"Oh darling," I said to her. "No one hates mornings more than me. No one has been an enemy of morning longer than your mother."

It then also occurred to me that perhaps the universe is sending these teen/tweens of mine exactly the mother they need. Perimenopausal as I am. I may be wildly deluding myself, but it keeps my head out of the oven. And all is well.

Here is another surprising upside about aging if, as I was, you were an average-looking kid. When I was thirty-eight, people said, "Oh, you look about forty. Are you forty?" It would freak me out and drive me to weeping on my own bed. But now that I'm more than fifty, people say I look pretty good. All my life I've looked about forty-two, and now I'm reaping the benefits. Sometimes I like to tell people I'm seventy just to get their enthusiastic and amazed reactions.

I believe it is a gift of the age that we live in that we have the luxury of looking at age as a construction. Because in contrast to every earlier milestone birthday (ten, twenty, thirty, and forty), my fiftieth was the most fun birthday of my life. So I've henceforth decided my fifties will be the fun decade. I am just so weary of the imposed tedium of adulthood. People always say, "Fifty is the new thirty-eight." "Why settle for thirty-eight? Thirty-eight is but another low-fat-yogurt-type form of sensible compromise. For next year, 'Maybe fifty-one is the new eleven!'"

I think of this and feel a bouquet of party balloons lifting into the wide blue sky.

And I'm reminded of the quote that Clare recently sent me (via Pablo Picasso via Jane Fonda): "It takes a long time to learn to be young."

Menopause Tips

THIS IS NOT TECHNICALLY an advice book, à la *Menopause for Dummies*. But some direct advice is perhaps needed. Here goes:

Women of this certain age need a particularly wide berth of compassion because of the extremes they may find themselves experiencing. I mean, since the beginning of time, people have had moods, sure, but menopause sets a totally different bar.

Saying a woman may have ups and downs during menopause is like calling Sylvia Plath a tad skittish. It's like trying to cover a bell jar with a tea cozy.

It's like saying Janis Joplin would have been okay if she had only drunk eight glasses of water a day and had been really firm about hydrating.

It's like saying Medea would have been fine if she had just done "this amazing ten-week Groupon course I just got Tweeted, about combining Pilates with restorative yoga!" ("And hey, have you tried this great Whole Foods shade-grown cham-

omile tea?"*Fuck off!*) Like Jason's nettlesome ex, men in litera-
ture have also had some legendarily dark moods. One thinks of
Mr. Kurtz (*Heart of Darkness*) and Captain Ahab (*Moby-Dick*).
However, note that unlike Medea, neither was a title character.
Oh no, their books were named after (1) a river (more or less)
and (2) a whale. How telling.

So herewith for the beleaguered (and those who love them)
are some handy menopause tips. This is non-sugar-coated,
boots-on-the-ground advice from the field, from women who
themselves have survived the change. That's right, people. This
is for real.

FOR YOUR elucidation, I recently met one more time with Dr.
Valerie, she of the ingenious Chinet-girls-vs.-paper-plate-girls
comparison. ("I only have about four good metaphors, and
that's one of them," she chuckles.) That said, Dr. Valerie did not
recommend *The Wisdom of Menopause* only because she hasn't
read it—her experience is based on several decades of her own
practice. For ease of reading, I conflated Dr. Valerie and Christiane Northrup because I found that what we are really looking for in this time are mother figures—sensible, smart, loving,
emotionally balanced tribal "elders" (although in fact Dr. Valerie is not old at all) who can describe to us how all can be well.

Dr. Valerie is always one to utter a faint and carefully polite
"Aha!" at any mention of chakras, but she also betrays her pro-
fessional medical bias when she suddenly starts exclaiming,
"Footnotes! If a book doesn't have many footnotes citing rig-

orously documented long-term medical studies, don't believe a word they say!"

So okay. Suffice it to say that, although references are mentioned, this book does not have a bible of footnotes, so take all with a grain of salt. That said, Dr. Valerie also says: "You have to laugh. This time of life is just so weird. And who knows everything, in the end?"

So in fact we were able to agree on a general philosophy.

Here's how the dream gynecologist would treat you (if you don't happen to have one nearby). They should not immediately prescribe any one-size-fits-all set of pills, treatments or another. Ideally he or she would listen to you for about an hour, with tissues, as you describe the panoply of emotional and physical issues that are occurring. I believe the length of time alone is important therapy.

The gynecologist would then deliver the equivalent of the Chinet-vs.-paper-plate speech. Which is to say yes, things are going on with you hormonally that make you feel unstable, but in midlife you may also have a lot on your plate that contributes to this sense of instability. So let's slow down and look at both. (Admits Dr. Valerie as a footnote, however: "Some women are like Eeyore, you know, they're anxious. Even if everything is perfect they will always need medication of some kind. Those are the women to whom I do not deliver the Chinet speech.")

The choice of treatment offered is between small, tweaked dosages of hormones ("You really have to be committed to monitoring it and tailoring it") taken for a limited period of time, low-level antidepressants taken for a limited period of time, or nothing at all ("When the feelings come on, just remember why they're happening, and notice them").

Rather than punishing dietary regimes, Dr. Valerie suggests considering becoming, as she is, a "flexatarian." A couple of days a week consider having a meatless meal, but don't go crazy.

Her wish overall: "I'd like women to grow middle-aged gracefully. Embrace being fifty."

So that's about strengthening the plate. As for taking things off one's plate, my humble menopause tips:

1. Free Yourself of Accustomed Relational Chores

Try on for size a fantastically freeing gambit called "Now That I'm Fifty" (or almost fifty—think of it as a happily metaphorical fifty). As my friend Denise puts it, "Now that I'm fifty, I don't visit my fighting in-laws in Cleveland anymore. My husband can go off and see them if he wants to, but I've been doing it for twenty years, and you know what? Never again. [Beat] I'm fifty!"

2. Free Yourself of Accustomed Domestic Chores

This is a gambit of my own invention that I call "Stuff It, Barbara Ehrenreich." Your own version may be different, but this was mine. Part of my own problem with home care was that for years I was afraid to hire domestic help, because Barbara Ehrenreich wrote in *Nickel and Dimed* that to have a Third World woman scrub your toilets is to oppress a fellow sister. But now that I can afford it, not often but enough, I've come out of denial over the fact that to have a house cleaned professionally is unbelievably fantastic. Once every two weeks

I bring in Marta—whom I refer to sometimes as Marta, and sometimes, baldly, as "the maid"—and when I do so, I silently flip Barbara Ehrenreich the finger. I'm fifty!

3. Accept the Chaos (If It Doesn't Drive You Nuts)

That said, while my own house is now in much better shape, not for show to the outside world but because it was literally driving me crazy, I am resigned to never having a cleaned-up car. My middle-aged menopausal Volvo is an old-enough family friend that she is allowed to remain who she is. In one of our semiannual sweeps, the girls and I made a really concerted effort to totally clean out the trunk, really and truly this time. By being so thorough, suddenly all over town we were finding ourselves without a sweater or without the bottom part of a ten-year-old's swimsuit or without that sometimes suddenly appreciated Costco twelve-pack flat of beef jerky. Which is to say we had forgotten how used we had become to feeding homeless people out of the back of my car. As opposed to a dollar bill, which I sometimes may or may not have handy, my daughters and I have found that homeless people requesting aid at stoplights may also happily accept a FUZE energy drink or a yogurt bar or a bag of Fritos, but interestingly, to the last man or woman, will *not* accept a V8.

4. Cut All Corners Possible, and Don't Apologize

I would say, unless you love it, let the Christmas-card thing go. Who really wants them anymore? Particularly not in June. It's absolutely all right that you didn't send them out on time, and you don't need to send an extra note apologizing. For God's sake. Let's not and say you did. Give yourself a friggin' break. Cut some corners already.

5. Don't Judge. Lower the Bar

Maybe you're just not a good sleeper. Take Ambien if you need to. Don't berate yourself. It's not for life. You just have to get through this stage/phase of life.

The stage I'm referring to, for many, is this sandwich-generation thing, which is no joke. We have to truly and deeply acknowledge that the care units we are taking on would crack not one but five Chinet plates. Which is to say that all bets are off now, and I mean all. There are no conventionally agreed-upon standards that make sense here. Sometimes a few eggs will roll out of the carton and simply crack, "one handed catch," whoops, no. Sometimes that squalling elder may have to suffer through a whole weekend—a whole weekend!—with the wrong kind of medical tights. Sometimes dinner for the kids will be mashed potatoes on biscuits with rice served in front of a sixth rerun of *SpongeBob* (a show that I believe, as with many of the new shows the kids love, is at least linguistically clever).

Sure, it would be nice to be sitting down to a home-cooked sit-down dinner with the whole family every night, with fresh plateware and glassware and folded cloth napkins, but if it doesn't happen, why blame it on the mothers? If America cares so much about the family dinner hour, let the Republicans get that family dinner on the table. Or Crate and Barrel.

6. Bed Rest: Lots of It

The medical advice will be all about hydrating and walking

and yoga, but sometimes all that simply adds up to more exhausting tasks—more things one must do that are good for one but do not give one pleasure, and indeed, too many of which make one dread the day. You are very fragile right now and can't take any more weight on either your paper or even Chinet plate. And honestly—stop the presses!—I don't think personal training is all that it's cracked up to be.

An enormously freeing thing is to see how long you can stay in bed. Read in bed, work in bed, watch TV in bed, eat in bed, sleep in bed (if you can sleep). It is wonderful to commit on, say, a Saturday, to just staying in bed.

If people ask you what you're doing, say: "I'm in menopause. One of the recommended cures is bed rest." I'm serious! When you really get bored with it, you will get out of bed—eventually. But why rush it?

7. Therapy May Not Be a Complete Solution

Beyond refereeing difficult conversations between spouses, as perhaps a priest or rabbi would, I believe therapists can be limited in how they can help. It is but one utensil in setting one's entire perimenopause table. It's not their fault. We pay them to be reasonable. By the time you've driven to his or her office and gotten your little ticket for parking and flicked the light switch and sat quietly on a wicker chair in the waiting room drinking chamomile tea and reading *Shambala* magazine, it's as though the problem is somehow containable, and it's really not. Therapists have the most carefully choreographed work schedules in the world ("I have Tuesday at 5:30 P.M. or Thursday at 8:00 A.M."), they watch the clock like hawks, they're rarely available for naked drumming—why do we bother with them? No amount of dialogue or intellect is going to solve some of these big kundalini-rising midlife problems. My old therapist urged me to live alone for a while before moving in with Mr. Y. Good advice, sure, but she wasn't the head of my village, I was madly in love, and the whole thing was going to come apart when it was going to come apart anyway. Therapists can't talk you out of a train wreck that's on its way—sometimes you just have to go through the crash and see if you can walk away on two legs.

They can help with the mother stuff. But it's not rocket science and you don't need a PhD, nor do you need fourteen hours of therapy to set up the backstory. You can also help yourself by breathing and just letting the grief wash over you.

8. Consider Everything and Anything to Get You Through This Passage

When you hit the midlife shoals, I'm going to recommend that you read everything, have a séance, do the tarot, maybe look into some past lives, get a gypsy lover. . . . Try everything. A close girlfriend of mine who is highly left-brained—she is a pharmacologist—at one point was trying to have a baby at forty-one. Times were desperate. It looked as if it was not going to happen. She was hysterical. She ended up, on a lark, going to a Vedic astrologer. She talked, cried, asked questions. The Vedic astrologer listened and consulted her chart. Suddenly she said: "What—oh! I see five little children here who will come to you with their suitcases already packed."

Thanks to her siblings, she ended up having two nephews and three nieces, who chatter on the phone with one another every week and whom she has had a total ball being an involved aunt to, without having to do the daily grunt work. In short, suitcases packed! A therapist is never going to come up with that in a million years.

Which is to say in the end, probably the biggest, and related, survival tip, though, is to have no shame. The middle-aged women I know, clawing their way one day at a time through this passage, have no rules—they glue themselves together with absolutely anything they can get their hands on.

They do estrogen cream, progesterone biocompounds, vaginal salves, coffee in the morning, big sandwiches at lunch.

They drink water all day, they work out twice a week, hard, with personal trainers.

They take Xanax to get over the dread of seeing their personal trainers, they take Valium to settle themselves before the first chardonnay of happy hour.

They may do with just a half a line of coke before a very small martini, while knitting and doing some crosswords.

If there are cigarettes and skin dryness, there are also collagen and Botox, and the exhilaration of flaming an ex on Facebook.

And finally, as another woman friend of mine counseled with perfect sincerity and cheer: "Just gain the twenty-five pounds. I really think I would not have survived menopause—*and* the death of my mother—without having gained these twenty-five pounds."

Sure, we're supposed to take calcium pills to avoid brittle bones and hip injuries at ninety, but who worries about living long when we're just trying to get through the day? In the end the *real* wisdom of menopause may lie in questioning how fun or even sane this chore wheel called modern life actually is.

And I must tell you, as a middle-aged woman who labors mightily—and fails even more mightily—every day to wear the mask of being sane, to admit to experiencing only the narrowest spectrum of emotions, from good-humored cheer to only the lightest irritation, a mood soothed easily with a good chuckle thanks to NPR—that it is beyond delicious.

Better to just hurl those coffee mugs straight out the window.

And if what works is black cohosh tea with a vodka chaser, and an overturned Greek tragedy mask as a chocolate-fondue fountain, then bottoms up! Avast, ye vampires and werewolves and pirates! *Arrr!*

It's a mad time of life.

And trust me, as one who has lived the miracle:

It really will get better.

Acknowledgments

A<small>LTHOUGH MOST OF THE</small> men who inspired this book's composite male characters might rightly want to seek refuge in various witness-protection programs, I want to single out and thank first and foremost Ben "master refinancer" Schwarz, who appears on page 1. My longtime editor at the *Atlantic*, Ben was urging me to write the source material for this book years before I was actually flood-spotting and spot-flooding. He was tireless in pushing me to get it right—I remember many editorial phone conferences that actually took place while I was waiting for the Volvo to be serviced. Due to his remarkable brilliance, care, and attention, Ben is the sort of magazine editor who comes but once a century—thank you.

Thanks, too, to my brother Eugene and his family, whose lovely Pacific Grove home I breezily tend to treat as a second one whenever I'm writing (or not). Thanks also to my friend of several decades now, Dan Akst. Wailed I at Pirate's Cove: "I used to feel really on top of it. I think I was super together around thirty-five. But the older I get, the stupider I feel. It seems more and more like I know absolutely nothing!" Replied Dan: "Don't worry. You're not getting stupider. It's just that

your perception of yourself is finally catching up to reality."
Hilarious, witty, true.

Other men who have been golden in times of stress: John
"June gloom be gone" Fleck, Carlos Rodriguez, and Dave (Mr.
Q) Zobel (trading "one-handed catches" with David Coons).

It's a cliché to say one could not have made it through certain life crises without one's girlfriends, but for me that's so to
the nth degree. The icing on the cake is that aside from mothers, daughters, artists, geniuses, and renegades, I know some of
the world's greatest writers, who provide hope that eventually
the chaos will have a narrative shape. As some of my girlfriends
whose fleeting imprints appear in this book may themselves be
seeking a witness-protection program, I thank all obliquely but
specifically: Anny C. and Danette C. (New Orleans Mardi Gras
joy division), Kate C. (surprise fiftieth-birthday-party division),
Rebecca C. (for, God, the AeroBed), Donna D. (who literally
keeps my family in Playboy binders), Samantha D. (who knows
a thing or two about tumult), Janet F. (who always makes us feel
heroic, because she is), Caitlin F. (car mitt/cleaning supplies,
queen frame and mattress still in plastic, grief counseling),
Karen F. and Maria D.H. (fellow Malibu Park Junior High
survivors), Annabelle G. (just because), Jude J. (of the perfect
English muffins), Gina K. (of iced Grey Goose and emergency
blow-up mattresses), Irene L. (I see us living together and going
to a lot of theater eventually), Kerry "Fightin' Writin' Mom"
M., Susan M. (cosmopolitans, shoe closet, "Estrogen Mood
and Memory Formula"), Beverly O. (my home away from
home), Joanne "School Mom" (big quotes) P., Rachel R. (for
those yelling-over-desert-sand calls from Burning Man), Erika

"Dusty Nethers" S. (too marvelously complex to reference in parentheses), Kaelyn S. (literally first on life's speed-dial), Mona S. (whose notable proverb about men in bow ties still haunts), Deb "Barn Dance" (big quotes) V., and Spike W. (who practices literally the "art" of menopause). Chiropractor Deb Yerman has also been a lifesaver (TMJ!).

In their own special enigmatic category of life fun, I thank, always, David Schweizer and Frier McCollister.

As Julie Andrews herself is not available for life counseling, I am so grateful to have met and subsequently interviewed the wonderful gynecologist Dr. Valerie Myers of Pasadena, whose calm and enduring wisdom inspires this book.

If I cannot have Pema Chödrön to call every Monday at 8:00, I am delighted to call my kick-ass sister, Tatjana, who has yet to collect royalties on the character of Kaitlin, whom she inspired.

This book would not have happened, of course, without the amazing Jill Bialosky.

BUT MOST of all, my heart belongs to my daughters, who made me find my smile. Only they will know what bad television we've watched together that that phrase is based on; they will giggle, and I do love the sound of that laughter.

MEMOIR

New York Times Book Review 100 Notable Books of the Year

In a voice that is wry, disarming, and totally candid, Sandra Tsing Loh tells the moving and laugh-out-loud tale of her roller coaster through "the change." This is not your grandmother's menopause story. Loh chronicles utterly relatable, everyday perils: raising preteen daughters, weathering hormonal changes, and the ups and downs of a career and a relationship. She writes also about an affair and the explosion of her marriage, while managing the legal and marital hijinks of her eighty-nine-year-old dad. The upbeat conclusion: it does get better.

"Reads like a weekend away with the best friend you ever had—
blazingly vulnerable, scorchingly smart, and funny as hell."
—Cheryl Strayed, author of *Wild*

"Loh here goes bravely into the mystery, which is
every memoir's mystery. How did I get this way? . . . [It] does what
memoir ought to do: it reminds the reader she's not alone."
—*Los Angeles Review of Books*

"[Reading this book] I laughed maniacally, nodded in empathy, hooted,
teared up, and laughed some more."—Mary Roach, author of *Gulp*

"Loh is such an engaging writer she manages to make this
extremely difficult time hilarious." —*New York Times Book Review*

Writer/performer Sandra Tsing Loh is a contributing editor to *The Atlantic*, host of the syndicated radio show *The Loh Down on Science*, and the author of five previous books. She lives in Pasadena, California.

Cover photographs (front) © Simon Lee; (back) WEKWEK/
Getty Images
Cover design by Chin-Yee Lai

W. W. NORTON
NEW YORK • LONDON
www.wwnorton.com

ISBN 978-0-393-35109-5

9 780393 351095

51595

$15.95 USA $18.95 CAN.